Noble Savage Cooking
Food and Manners for a Corrupt Civiliz

MW00901521

By:
Chef Dave Bridges

This Book is dedicated to my wife Stephanie and my girls, Lily Helene and Madeleine Laura. Never be afraid to take the path less traveled.

Table of Contents

CHAPTER 1: Libations and Cracklins

The Significance of Proper Bartending

In good times people want to drink. In bad times people have to.

How many seconds does it take for the warm blanket of bliss to cover your body after the first sip of a properly crafted cocktail? It's pure and natural bliss gives you a feeling of comfort and pleasure. It is a sense of being and belonging in your own world. It is the knowing that things are good. Hell, by the time the glass is nothing but a few naked ice cubes, things may very well be great. The first sip of the first drink is just that--a first impression. I would not advise anyone to risk such an important role in the psyche of not only himself but his guests to substandard bartending.

One cannot and should not underestimate the significance of knowing how to properly craft a real cocktail. Even in the world of the professional restaurant it is often an overlooked after thought to providing you an entertaining evening. What has the world come to when the "bartender" can make every blue, purple, green drink and red drink while juggling 4 bottles of Schnapps and setting his nose hair on fire? But you ask for a Side Car and get a look as blank as Kristen Stewart's personality. I continually strive everyday to be a better person and to help people be upstanding stalwarts of their community. In the same ways that cuisine brings people together, so equally does drink.

Think of a good drink in the same way you would think of authentic Japanese food. Very few ingredients are used. Therefore, each ingredient must be of the highest level. Don't buy any alcohol that comes in a plastic bottle. You will save yourself a world of headache, literally, by not drinking anything presented to you in such an abomination. The only thing they are putting in there to make "gin" is the ability to heighten your poor judgment.
Buy alcohol from the countries that it is supposed to come from. In the same way that you would never eat Etouffee in New Jersey, you should never buy Cognac from Cleveland.

Since there are so few things that make a fine cocktail, you must be precise at measurements. Say you have 2 ounces of brandy and 2 ounces of Cointreau in the recipe. You get sloppy and lazy by pouring 1 1/2 ounces of brandy and 2 1/2 ounces of Cointreau. You have just changed the taste of the libation by 25%! "I'm sorry Mr. Bridges, but we can't pay you the money as promised by 25%". Unacceptable.

Every type of glass has a size and a shape for a reason. My personal build is a bit robust with a slight taller than average height. I am built that way so that I can accommodate my appetite for life. A champagne glass is designed to concentrate the bubbles straight up to tickle your lip. A rocks glass should have a very heavy bottom in order to withstand the muddler and help keep it upright on the bar as you get a little free spirited. Specific glasses have been designed for specific drinks for 150 years. Instead of diluting your valuable time into trying to figure out why, just accept it and fall back on 150 years of research, tradition and accidents.

Ice should be of the large variety. It is a fact that larger cubes melt slower than the smaller ones. The idea is to chill your drink, not water it down. If you want to know the scientific molecular reasoning, send Harold McGee an email. I have seen some online stores where you could purchase ice trays that make larger ice cubes. You could also take a bread loaf pan and just freeze a large block to which you wield a fabulous ice pick. Very manly, very butch, chicks really dig that.

The techniques should not be taken for granted either. If is says "shake", then shake. If it says "stir", then stir. Assuming a lackadaisical approach to the techniques of crafting a cocktail will just lead to a very uninspiring result. It would be like butchering the motions of the Tango only to dip the girl in the end and think she is actually still going to desire you. Take each technique seriously. It will show your work in an honest and naked fashion in the end.
Everything that finds itself upon your palate is better fresh. You would never in your life take an asparagus out of the can and put it on your salad plate. If you would, then stop here and please just give my tome of knowledge to someone else. Bottled lemon juice is nasty. I know it says "Real" on the label. But if I squeeze a lemon and leave the juice on the counter, eventually it starts to bubble and fizz. I could leave that "Real" stuff on the counter as an heirloom to my grand children and it would taste and act in the same way as the day I let its filthy personality into my home. Use fresh ingredients and the summer sun will always shine your way.

Do things with Flair. For the love of God, when I say "Flair", I'm not talking about the juggling bartender with the faux hawk and the shirt so tight I can tell you where he cut himself manscaping. I am talking about style. Take each action and make it with just a touch more drama. Pour the liquor into the glass from a few inches higher than normal. Shake the cocktail up high and over your shoulder as if you were Carmen Miranda at the CoCo Cabana. Drop the in the lemon peel with the flourish of the hands of David Copperfield. Be slightly dramatic. You're here to have fun, so make it that way and your guests will follow suit.

Lillet Refresher with Salmon Cracklins
Serves 4

There are times when you may want to give the appearance of being slightly more sophisticated than you actually may be. Nothing does that better than ordering something French that nobody has hardly ever heard of. Step up to the bar and let the romanticism of France roll off your tongue, *"Lillet Blanc"*. Lillet Blanc is a wonderful L'aperitif with hints of orange and honey. This refresher will keep you cool and satiated. Looking all the while, that you are indeed the sum of all your parts.

Lillet Refresher
1 Bottle Lillet Blanc
1 liter Ginger Ale
1 orange cut into slices for garnish as well as flavor

Use a traditional rocks glass and over fill it with large ice cubes. Fill the glass half way with the Lillet Blanc, its your choice to which half of the glass you want to fill. Fill the remaining vacant half of the glass with the Ginger Ale. Squeeze one slice of orange and drop into the drink. Stir the drink one time with your finger. Repeat 3 more times or do all 4 glasses at once like any normal person.

Salmon Cracklins
Salmon Skin from one side of fresh salmon
Corn Starch for dusting
Coarse Sea Salt
Fennel Pollen

Pre-heat your deep fat fryer to 350 degrees. Cut the skin of the salmon into 1-inch strips. Lightly toss the skin in some cornstarch and shake off any excess cornstarch. Place the skin into the fryer one strip at a time and fry in batches of 10 -12 strips. Fry each batch until the skin is lightly brown and the skin in the fryer has refrained from popping at you any more. Remove the skin from the fryer and place on a paper towel to absorb any of the excess oil. While the skin is still hot sprinkle with the salt and fennel pollen.

****Creoles believe that when you cut a cucumber, you must cut the stem end first and then rub it against the spot it was just cut from. This is said to take the bitterness or the "fever" from a cucumber.

Molasses Whiskey Smash with Pork Gratons
Serves 4

One fine evening I was truly being entertained at the bar of the Renaissance Hotel in New Orleans by Chris McMillian, a true master of the craft. Every single cocktail Chris makes is absolute perfection. However, perfection does take time.

So if you're in a rush to escape your immediate mental surroundings, don't go see Chris. But if you are curious to see just how true bartending is preformed at the highest level, before some 21 year old bottle juggling circus act ruins it for the next generation, find Chris. Order this drink and pay attention as he wields the bar shaker while simultaneously weaving the most beautiful poem on Bourbon you have ever heard.

Molasses Whiskey Smash
2 Lemons (cut into halves, then cut each half into quarters)
8 sprigs of Fresh Mint
4 ounce Molasses
1 Bottle Fine Kentucky Bourbon such as Makers Mark

Place 3 of the quartered lemon pieces into a Boston Shaker glass with 1 sprig of mint and 1 ounce of molasses. Muddle the ingredients in the glass. Place a few large cubes of ice into the shaker glass and pour in a shot or so of Bourbon. Shake the glass a good 15 times and strain into a rocks glass that is over flowing with ice. Garnish your beverage with a piece of lemon and one sprig of mint.

Pork Gratons
1lb piece of Pork Belly with the skin still attached
Creole Seasoning

Pre-heat your deep fryer to 225 degrees. Cut the pork belly into 1 1/2 inch cubes. Fry the pork for 15-20 minutes until the pork is browned nicely. Remove the gratons from the fryer and lay on a paper towel and let cool for a good 20 minutes. Raise the heat of your fryer to a blistering 400 degrees. Place the pork back into the fryer and fry until you see the skin blister and get yummy, crunchy crackly. Remove from the fryer onto a paper towel and liberally sprinkle the Creole Seasoning over the pork gratons.
OR, if the great gastronomic deity has laid his hand on your soul and you find yourself living in his land of South Louisiana. Just go to the nearest gas station and buy a bag already cooked for 8 bucks.

****Pork Gratons will stay good for days. I often keep them in a paper bag in my car for the week, just eating a little here or there, especially whenever I get cut off.

The Zenith of Man's Pleasure

"Then comes the zenith of man's pleasure.
Then comes the julep – the mint julep.
Who has not tasted one has lived in vain.
The honey of Hymettus brought no such solace to the soul;
the nectar of the gods is tame beside it.
It is the very dream of drinks,
the vision of sweet quaffings.

The Bourbon and the mint are lovers.
In the same land they live,
on the same food are they fostered.
The mint dips its infant leaf
into the same stream
that makes the Bourbon what it is.
The corn grows in the level lands
through which small streams meander.
By the brook-side the mint grows.
As the little wavelets pass,
they glide up to kiss the feet of the growing mint,
and the mint bends to salute them.
Gracious and kind it is,
living only for the sake of others.
Like a woman's heart
it gives its sweetest aroma when bruised.
Among the first to greet the spring, it comes.
Beside the gurgling brooks that make music in the fields,
it lives and thrives.
When the bluegrass begins to shoot its gentle sprays to sun,
mint comes, and its sweetest soul drinks at the crystal brook.
It is virgin then.
But soon it must be married to old Bourbon.
His great heart, his warmth of temperament,
and that affinity which no one understands,
demands the wedding.

How shall it be?

Take from the cold spring some water,
pure as angels are;
mix it with sugar till it seems like oil.
Then take a glass
and crush your mint within it with a spoon
– crush it around the borders of the glass
and leave no place untouched.

Then throw the mint away
– it is a sacrifice.
Fill with cracked ice the glass;

pour in the quantity of Bourbon which you want.
It trickles slowly through the ice.
Let it have time to cool,
then pour your sugared water over it.
No spoon is needed;
no stirring allowed
– just let it stand a moment.
Then around the brim place sprigs of mint,
so that the one who drinks may find taste and odor at one draft.

"Then when it is made, sip it slowly.
August suns are shining,
the breath of the south wind is upon you.
It is fragrant, cold and sweet – it is seductive.
No maiden's kiss is tenderer or more refreshing,
no maiden's touch could be more passionate.
Sip it and dream – you cannot dream amiss.
Sip it and dream – it is a dream itself.
No other land can give so sweet solace for your cares;
no other liquor soothes you in melancholy days

Sip it and say there is no solace for the soul,
no tonic for the body like old Bourbon whiskey."

Anonymous Journalist
Lexington Times
19th Century

Hendricks Martini and Fried Pickles
Serves 4

I really wasn't a gin drinker until I tried Hendricks. It has a lovely breath of cucumber that makes the gin feel as posh as touching a woman's smooth leg. While I personally may be not confident enough in my manhood to order a drink that comes in the same vessel that I have seen so many Cosmos and Appletinis. However, don't let my mental defects distract you from what is surely a celebration of life in liquid.

Hendricks Martini
1 bottle Hendricks Gin9
1 bottle Dry Vermouth
Handful of your favorite green olives

Take a Martini Glass and fill it with ice. Fill your cocktail shaker with ice. Start pouring the Hendricks into the shaker and count to 6. Place the top onto the shaker and shake vigorously 50 solid times. Fell free to do the shaking into the air and over your shoulder for a huge show that your friends will never forget. Make sure the top of the shaker is fastened securely or you will be creating a memory that will be tough to ever overcome. Dump the ice out of your glass and pour a ½-ounce of dry vermouth into your glass. Swirl the Vermouth around the glass and dump it out. Place a few olives into the glass and pour the gin into the glass. Only if you have shaken the gin a vigorous 50 times will the magic layer of ice appear on top of the martini. Repeat 3 more times for your guests and 1 more time for yourself.

Fried Pickles
Dill pickles sliced in any sort of fashion
2 cups flour
1 Tablespoon Kosher salt
1 egg
1 cup milk

Pre-heat a deep fryer to 350 degrees. Place the flour into bowl and season with the salt. In a separate bowl, marry the egg and the milk until it is one smooth mixture. Take 10 or so slices of pickle and dredge into the flour. Then place the dredged pickles into the egg wash. Remove the pickles from the egg wash and dredge again in the flour. Place the pickles into the fryer and fry until lightly golden. Carefully take the pickles out of the fryer and lay onto a paper towel. Place onto a dish and serve with the martinis. Be very mindful to let the pickles cool a bit unless someone you are serving has previously made your ears burn.

"Never trust a man that wears a bow tie or drinks out of a straw."
Me

Sazerac with Candied Cracklins
Serves 4

I cannot begin to explain the gastronomic ledge I have thrust myself onto by attempting to publish a recipe for the Sazerac. It is akin to any passionate discussion on BBQ or Gumbo or the Presidency. No matter what you say, somebody is going to get their panties all tied up in a wad. In the darkness, I have included the "options" below and you can find the light on your own.
One thing is for certain: Do not use Bourbon EVER. That would just be a sure sign of poor breeding.

Sazerac
Sugar Cubes
Peychaud bitters
Angostura bitters
1 bottle Rye Whiskey

1 Bottle of Absinthe or Herbsaint
4 strips of Lemon peel

Fill a rocks glass with ice and set aside. Place the sugar cube with just enough water to moisten it into another rocks glass and crush the sugar. Add 4 dashes of Peychauds, 1 DROP of Angostura and 2 ounces of Rye whiskey into the glass with the crushed sugar. Place a few cubes of ice into the glass with the Whiskey and stir 4 or 5 times to chill. Remove and discard the ice from the first glass. Pour 1/2 ounce of Absinthe or Herbsaint into the chilled glass, turning to perfume the entire inside of the glass. Relieve the glass of the excess Absinthe or Herbsaint. Strain the whiskey into the perfumed glass. Take a piece of your lemon peel and rub the outer portion of the peel over the rim of the glass. Then twist the peel over the top of the drink allowing the oils of the lemon to mist the face of the Sazerac. Don't commit the sin of dropping the peel into the drink. Serve.

Candied Cracklins
Pork rind pellets or 1 commercial bag of fried spicy pork rinds
Creole seasoning
Steens cane syrup

Heat your deep fryer to 360 degrees. Sprinkle some of those magical pork rind pellets into the fryer and fry until all are puffed and crispy. Make sure you stir the pellets well and they are completely puffed. An uncooked or even partially cooked pork rind is a certain recipe for a smile tainted with a chipped tooth. Remove the puffed pork rinds from the fryer onto a paper towel and liberally season the rinds with your favorite Creole seasoning. Place a large skillet on top the stove over medium heat. Pour enough cane syrup into the pan to cover the bottom by 1/2 inch. Bring to a simmer and cook for 4-5 minutes. Remove the pan from the stove and stir in one layer of pork rinds. Coat the rinds with the syrup. Place the rinds on some wax paper or a non-stick pan to cool. Once cool, serve with the Sazeracs.

****Cleaning a pan that used to hold caramel is difficult to clean to say the least. Fill the pan with water and bring it to a boil. The stuck cane syrup pieces will come right off in a snap.

Side Car with Fried Hominy
Serves 4

This is my all time favorite transition drink. After wasting all too many of my youthful years on cheap rum and coke, only to follow that up with screwdrivers, which turned out to be an even larger corruption of my innocence. "Adult Dave" was born the moment my friend Lu Brow from Cafe Adelaide poured me the most perfect blend of maturity disguised as a Side Car. Classically, the libation is served "up" in a martini glass. But as I explained in the martini recipe, I cannot drink out of one of those vessels. Although, I do make an exception in the allowance of a sugared rim. Go figure!

Side Car
Sugar
1 orange sliced thinly
1 bottle of Hennessy Cognac VSOP
1 bottle of Cointreau
1 cup fresh squeezed lemon juice

Pour a ½-inch layer of sugar onto a small salad size plate. Take one of the slices of orange and rub the cut flesh across the rim of the glass. Invert the glass and mount the rim onto the layer of sugar. Give the glass a few twists into the sugar in the same way you nestle your foot into the sand at the beach. Remove the glass from the sugar and place the orange slice into the glass. Over fill the glass with large ice cubes. Pour one portly shot of both the Cognac and the Cointreau into the glass. Pour 3/4 of an ounce of lemon juice into the glass. Give it 3 gentle stirs and serve.

Fried Hominy
1 10 ounce can of Hominy
1 Tablespoon chile powder
1 Tablespoon ground cumin
1 teaspoon cayenne powder
1 teaspoon powdered garlic
Kosher or Sea Salt
chopped cilantro

Pre-heat a deep fryer to 350 degrees. Expose the hominy by removing the lid of the can. Drain the hominy thoroughly and pat dry then submerge it into the deep fryer. You may need to stir the hominy in the fryer to keep them segregated. Fry for 5 to 6 minutes or until the hominy is brown and not so insistent on spitting at you from inside the fryer any more. Remove the hominy from the fryer and place in a medium sized stainless steel bowl. Liberally season the fried nuggets with the salt, spices and cilantro. Toss into the air 7 or 8 times and place into a dish for everyone to snack.

****You should always season fried foods when they come fresh out of the fryer. The heat will help the seasoning adhere.

Bloody Mary "Bubble Tea" with Nuts
Serves 4

The quintessential Sunday late morning hang over drink. The Bloody Mary has legions of fans and just as many variations. The devotees swear by the medicinal and almost black magic properties that the beverage possesses in exercising the demons from your head. It instills a vigor back into one's step and gets you ready for yet another day of reveling right when you thought another day's worth of sin was too much. Feel free to substitute into the garnishes any number of vegetables and pickles or even a boiled shrimp and a raw oyster for that extra potency that one might require in the latter era of HIS life.

Bloody Mary
1 bottle Fine Vodka
1 bottle Tomato juice
1 bottle Tabasco
1 bottle Worcestershire
1 jar prepared Horseradish
2 Lemons cut into halves
Sea or Kosher Salt
Fresh cracked Black Pepper
Firm Veal Demi-Glace cut into 1/2 inch cubes
1 jar of each Pickled Okra, Pickled Green Beans, Pickled Quail Eggs
4 stalks of Celery

Pour 2 ounces of vodka into a highball glass that is over flowing with ice. Add 3 ounces of tomato juice to the glass with 4 dashes of Tabasco, 2 dashes of Worcestershire, 1 teaspoon horseradish, the juice of half a lemon and a pinch of salt and pepper. Use a long spoon and stir very well. Stir in 1/3 cup of your veal demi jewels. Impale okra, a few green beans and a quail egg with a cocktail pic. Place the highly decorated pic into your beverage and plant the celery stalk down into the ice. Place a large mouthed straw into the libation so that the luxury of the demi-glace and tickle your tongue. Serve and repeat as needed to help your guests revive their sense of good taste.

Crispy Nuts
Zatarains granulated Crab Boil
1 cup Raw Peanuts
1 cup Pistachios
1 cup Pecans
1 cup Whole Almonds
1 cup Cashews
1 Lemon
Leaves of the Celery

Pre heat your fryer to 360 degrees. Fry the nuts in batches for a few minutes until brown. Remove the nuts from the fryer and place into a large salad bowl. Season the nuts with a scant sprinkling of the Zatarains crab boil. Be careful because it get spicy fast. Once all of our nuts are seasoned and cooled. Grate the zest of your lemon over the nuts and throw in a handful of celery leaves. Toss again in the bowl and serve in something appropriate. By "serve in something appropriate" I mean the nuts, you can choose to be as inappropriate with your haberdashery as you wish.

****The Bloody Mary may be considered the queen of all hang over drinks. But if you drank quality liquor you probably would never had gotten the hang over to start.

Old Fashioned with a Cane Syrup Bacon Lollipop
Serves 4

One wonderful Wednesday morning I was presented with an Old Fashioned. The only thing I knew about the beverage was that Maw Maw really enjoyed it when ever we would go dine together. As a young adult with an even younger palate and yet an even younger level of maturity, I had not acquired a taste for whiskey. Like it or not, I am growing older and my culinary constitution can't seem to handle sweet drinks any more. This version lets you regulate the level of sweetness with a lollipop that has my favorite culinary ingredient in the world-- bacon. Let the Old Fashioned tickle your tongue, then suck on the lollipop until you are sucrose satisfied. How could one go wrong?

Old Fashioned
Sugar cubes
Peychaud Bitters
1 bottle of Dewers white label
1 lemon
1 orange
Cherries

Place one sugar cube into an Old Fashioned glass with 2 dashes of bitters and a teaspoon of water. Muddle and break up the sugar. Twist a piece of lemon peel and place it into the glass with a few large ice cubes. Pour in 2 ounces of Dewers and gently give the glass a few whirls with a spoon or your finger. Top with a cherry and a slice of orange. Serve. Repeat as many times as wanted or even needed.

Cane syrup Bacon Lollipop
1 cup sugar
1/2 cup Steens Cane syrup
1/4 cup of water
2 strips of crispy cooked bacon, finely chopped

Spray some lollipop molds with non-stick spray. Lay the lollipop sticks in the molds and place the molds on a part of the counter that is not in use. Place the sugar, cane syrup and water into a small pot and place the pot over medium-high heat. Stir the mixture with a candy thermometer until the sugar is dissolved. Cook until the sugar reaches 300 degrees. Remove from the heat and stir in the bacon. Pour the mixture into your molds and let cool and set. Use the lollipops and the Old Fashioned as a reminder of how childhood was and how it should have been.

****If you don't own a muddler, then use the handle of a wooden spoon. If you don't have a wooden spoon then close the book and go buy one now.

Pimms Cup with Lemon and Anchovy Cracklins
Serves 4

Most often when I am traveling for pleasure and even for business, I go out in search of a new experience. New experiences come in episodes that tend to be both "good" and "bad". Being exposed to a different point of view on life can never be a wrong thing. One evening, I walked into the bar of Jacques-Imos restaurant. I figured there couldn't be a better place to order a drink that I had never had before in an establishment that was known highly for its fried chicken, shot drinking and Coyote Ugly bar dancing chef. Amongst the thickness of the New Orleans humidity, I sipped on my, oh so refreshing British Pimms Cup. I most certainly withdrew from the restaurant that night having experienced a totally new point of view on life that evening.

Pimms Cup
1 Bottle of Pimms No1 Cup
1 bottle Lemonade
1 bottle Club Soda
1 Cucumber
Sprigs of Mint

Fill a Collins glass with ice. Pour 2 ounces of Pimms into the glass with 2 ounces of lemonade. Stir a few vigorous times. Splash in an ounce of club soda and slide a slice of cucumber down in between the cubes of ice with a sprig or two of mint. Avoid all temptation to stir again. Repeat the process for as many people as you care to make happy.

Lemon and Anchovy Cracklins
1 lemon
8 white anchovies (plain anchovies will do if you are in a bind)
2 cups flour
1 tablespoon Kosher Salt
1 egg
1 cup milk

Pre-heat your deep fryer to 360 degrees. Slice the whole lemon from end to end paper thin. You may use a mandolin or a companion with proper knife skills. Choose what you must, as long as the lemon slices are cut "paper" thin. Ignore the inner child in you thinking that the peel and the seeds taste like crap. This is not the case. Mince the anchovies and spread around on the unadulterated slices of lemon. In a bowl, mix the flour with the salt. In a separate bowl, whisk the milk with the egg. Dredge the lemon slices into the flour until well coated. Then dip back into the egg wash and then dredge once more in the flour. Place the slices into the fryer and cook until golden. Drain the fried lemon on a paper towel and serve with a sprinkling of salt.

****In most occasions it is best to sit at the bar to eat. You don't need a reservation and the service is always spectacular. The bartender has nowhere to go.

D'Artagnan and Tabasco cured Bacon
Serves 2

Has anything in history with the christened name "D'Artagnan" fallen short of any less than the superlative adjective of "exemplary"? The D'Artagnan is a classic Champagne cocktail that contains a few liquors, some orange and a quality Champagne. You will not see it at your local "all you can drink for an extra $5.99" brunch, in the same way that you would not see me there either. Since it is morning and we are drinking, we might as well push all of our chips into the kitty and have a noshing of spicy bacon while we are at it.

D'Artagnan
1 bottle Fine quality Brandy
1 bottle Grand Marnier
2 Oranges cut into halves
Simple Syrup
1 bottle of good true Champagne

Fill a Boston Shaker half of the way with some ice. Pour in a 1 ounce of Brandy, 1 ounce of Grand Marnier, squeeze the juice of one of the orange halves into the shaker along with a splash of simple syrup. Stir very well and strain into a champagne flute. Top off your flute with the Champagne and garnish with a strip of orange peel.

Tabasco cured Bacon
1 pound of sliced Bacon
1 Bottle of Tabasco

Pre heat your oven to 375 degrees. Separate all the strips of bacon and place into a plastic sealable bag. Season the bacon with the Tabasco. Try to be as generous with the Tabasco as if it was your wallet and the bacon was a new love interest. If you don't understand what this means then you are probably single and your bacon will be unsatisfied. Let the bacon marinate in your cooler for 1 hour. Take the bacon out of the bag and lay it on a non-stick pan or a pan that is lined with metal foil. Bake the bacon until it is crispy. Remove the bacon from the pan and blot the excess grease dry with a paper towel. Serve your cooled bacon on anything. Bacon is such a loved vice that people will eat it off the back of a man dressed in corduroy if they have to.

****A voodoo love powder is a half teaspoonful of sugar, teaspoonful of peppermint and a teaspoonful of grated candied orange peel. Administering a teaspoonful of this mixture in a glass of wine would cause that person to love you forever.

Chapter 2 Head

The Significance of the Ghetto Market

Every city of any size has at least one ethnic market. You may not know where it is. Hell, you may even be in denial that it even exists in your city. But I'm here to tell you it's not only there, but it is glorious. Just put on your big boy pants, place your wallet in your front pocket, and take off all your jewelry and head to the hood. First of all, it's preferable to travel in the morning hours. It's during this time that most of the unsavory characters that congregate near the front door drinking malt liquor spiked beverages are usually still passed out from a long night of imbibing and throwing dice. Position your vehicle amongst the parking lot "gumbo" and make your way into the store. Remember; only through adversity, determination and danger can one ever find his true path as a cook.

Within the market lies an abundance of culinary treasures. Most prima donna chefs spend hours in an office on the Internet looking for exotic ingredients. They could have easily acquired these ingredients, for half the price, if they just had enough balls to drive where their dishwasher lives. Then again, if they were comfortable with the level of testosterone their body produces they would be on the line cooking. Not sitting in the office. But that's another story for another day.

The products within the market may vary greatly according to whichever ethnicity dominates the surrounding hood. But the underlying theme constantly remains the same: inexpensive cuts of proteins and organs prepped to be cooked in the traditions of the local grandmothers. You won't find beef tenderloin here. You will find land-roving verities such as beef tongue, pork liver, chicken feet and duck bills. On the shelves that carry the ocean delicacies, you can browse all types of mud dwellers and bottom feeders. Buffalo fish, catfish, crawfish and don't forget the shad roe, dried shrimp, mullet, gar and alligator sit side by side begging for a true accomplished cook to coax the sweet sea into dancing with the palate. All of these things can reach sublime delicacy levels in the hands of a real cook.

We often look at the ghetto market as a place for the "blue collar". We see it as a place where the base customers didn't quite see the climax of a high school education. Of course we see it in that skewed light. The food there is downright cheap. As Americans, we equate quality with price. Society instead should be placing more an emphasis on the relationship of price and skill level. The balance is as follows: the lower the price, the harder for "Susie Homemaker" to make palatable. In turn, the depth of flavor will be greatly higher. It is that exact balance that makes the ghetto market a refuge of cooks that are far more intelligent than any 2.5 child bearing Chevy Suburban driver. These cooks routinely take what the food society considers garbage and transforms it into gold. The braising, brining slow food movement may be new in today's haute cuisine restaurants. But in the ghetto, it has been a way of fashioning pleasure in an otherwise unpleasurable environment for many generations.

Thomas Keller said, "If I source out the best possible product, then I already have a head start on making a truly great dish". It is no secret anymore that all the "tougher" cuts of beef have far more flavor. So is it possible that the impoverished people of our country are already starting out with a better product than us? Walk that product hand in hand with their greater reliance on tradition and Susie Homemaker may just never catch up. The recipes that constitute the law of the ghetto market are from their grandmother's grandmother. How could anyone beat that? Even though all of our grandmothers had the same life obstacles we face today, we use those obstacles as a barrier to learning tradition and an excuse to make meals that make Rachel Ray a rich woman.

The current economic storm has forced the chefs of our country to be more creative with the lesser more inexpensive ghetto cuts of meat. In all honesty it kind of pisses me off. These ingredients in the proper hands of an accomplished chef will produce creations that are incredible—although still too expensive. Whereas, it will turn absolutely miserable in the hands of a cook that has ignored maw maw in favor of a young career full of foie gras, truffles and foam. Either way the price we all pay still goes up. A prime example is Bar B Que. The price of ribs just makes me sick. I don't think they really sell them anymore in the ghetto market. Ribs are following the same historical path as that cockroach of the sea, lobster. Once, lobster had to be regulated by the government in New England. It seems they were forcing the penal system inhabitants to eat too much lobster and that was considered to be inhumane. Now everyone knows how to cook it and the price reserves the sweet meat for only special occasions.

There are not many pleasures I have left in this world. But the ghetto market and the traditions that make up its foundation is one of them. As long as there are incompetent chefs and too busy to do anything other than complain housewives, I should be able to hold on to this one. But just like the good ole days of cheap ribs, lobster and pork bellies, deep in my heart I know the truth. The truth has a number nailed straight into the heart of it. That number is counting down the days before it bids me adieu.

Hog Head Cheese
Serves 10

One day I was having the most wonderful lunch of raw oysters and pork belly in San Francisco. I had seemed to turn into the world's best friend, especially after a bottle of proper Alsatian wine. Having completely been enraptured by my lunch, I decided to inform the chef of our newly formed brotherhood. I proceeded back into the kitchen with a glass of wine for my lost brother. After the initial shock and subsequent cursing from my brother (he must be from the temperamental French side of the family), we hashed out our lost imaginary childhood together over some more wine and bivalves. He apologized for cursing at me, as any real brother would, and told me it was just a case of mistaken identity. I had been mistaken for a man that just last week, snuck into the back alley of the kitchen and stole his Hog Head. I dreamed, what a spectacular city to live in, when one has to worry about their Hog Head being lifted!

Hog Head Cheese
1 Hog's Head
5 pig feet
1 Yellow Onion cut into quarters
5 stalks of Celery cut into large pieces
2 medium Carrots cut into large pieces
10 cloves Garlic
1 Tablespoon Red Pepper flakes
1 bunch of about 20 sprigs of fresh Thyme
1 bunch of about 10 sprigs of fresh Oregano
1 bunch of about 5 sprigs of fresh Sage
6 bay leaves
1/4 cup whole Black Peppercorns
1 bottle crisp White Wine
Sea or Kosher Salt
Favorite Creole Seasoning
1 cup chopped fresh Italian Parsley
1 bunch chopped green onion

Place your hog head in a very large pot. Tie the herbs together with a string and nestle into the mouth of the pig. Add all of the rest of the ingredients with 2 Tablespoons of both the salt and Creole seasoning. Fill the pot with water until it reaches a few inches above the head of the swine. Place the heavy pot on the stove over medium high heat and bring to a slow simmer. When you see the clouds of grey pollution float to the top. Carefully take a spoon and remove it from your presence. Gently coax the goodness out of your ingredients for 4 hours. If the water level dissipates to the point of reaching the top of your hog's head just add a bit more.

Turn off the heat and let the head cool in the stock. Remove the head and the feet from the pot and strain the liquid through a chinois or cheesecloth or even some sexy panty hose. Chill the stock over night.

Pick all of the meat from the head and the feet while they are warm and still in a giving mood. Place all of the meat into a mixing bowl being certain not to neglect the ears by omitting them. Throw some of the skin from the feet and the head in with the meat for good measure. Taste the gelatinous mixture and season as you wish with the creole seasoning and salt. Make sure the mixture is slightly saltier and spicy than you wish. The eventual chilling of the headcheese will mute the flavors. Set the meat aside.

Take your chilled stock and remove the solidified fat from the top of the stock. Save the fat for something fun on a later day with a loved one. Place the stock into a pot and reduce it by 2/3 over medium heat. Taste the stock for seasoning. Adjust your seasoning just as you did with the meat mixture.

Line the inside of a terrine mold with some plastic wrap. Making sure that the wrap over hangs the side of the terrine by at least a few inches. Add the Italian parsley and the scallion to the meat mixture. Pour just enough warm stock into the meat mixture for it to be as thick and moist as the people in the French Quarter on Mardi Gras Day. Fill the terrine mold with the meat mixture and lay the over hanging plastic wrap over the top of the warm headcheese. Chill the terrine over night.

Serve your Hog's Head Cheese by presenting thin slices to your friends with some freshly torn French bread. Place a slice on your tongue and close your eyes as the nature's gelatin dissolves across your palate.

"God Sends the Meat. The Devil Sends the Cooks"
T Deloney 1607

Grouper Cheeks with Brown Butter and Chicory
Serves 4

The cheeks of any animal are almost certain to be one of the best if not the best part of the whole beast. How do I know this to be fact? The butchers and fishermen save the prized cheeks for themselves. To be fair we are kind of making it easy for them. You never see a piece of TGI McFunster O'Mally's propaganda shoving endless bowls of boneless buffalo flavored fish cheeks in your face. So if you don't want to take it from me that the cheeks of any animal are the best. Then take it from the men and women whom are your butchers and fishmongers. They are by far more honest and morally upright than I could ever aspire to be. Not that I would ever aspire to be that way. After all, honest work is just that---honest work.

Grouper Cheeks with Brown Butter and Chicory
1 pound Grouper Cheeks
Flour
Sea or Kosher Salt
Freshly cracked Black Pepper

20

9 Tablespoons of cubed unsalted Butter
1/2 head of Chicory/Curly Endive/Frisee, cut out the core
16 or so fresh Tarragon leaves
1 Meyer Lemon or a Lemon with a scant touch of sugar

Season the cheeks with the salt and pepper on both sides. Powder your GROUPER cheeks, its best to be specific in this case, with some flour. Place a large skillet on your burner over medium-high heat with 1 Tablespoon of the butter. When your skillet is hot and the butter has succumb and covered the bottom of the pan add the cheeks. Cook for 2 minutes until the cheeks are golden brown on one side. Resist the urge to shake the pan like the idiots on the Gordon Ramsey show. Flip the cheeks and cook for another 2 minutes until golden brown again. Remove the cheeks from the pan and divide the bounty onto 4 separate plates. Place the skillet back onto the heat and add the remaining 8 ounces of butter. Swirl the butter in the pan as it fizzles and bubbles until it becomes light brown. Toss your Endive into the pan simultaneously adding the tarragon and a slight sprinkling of Salt and Pepper. After tossing the endive 5 or 6 times in the nutty butter, remove the pan from the heat. Squeeze the juice from your lemon into the pan and divide the Chicory and butter amongst the 4 plates. Serve immediately or stand in the kitchen eating all 4 dishes and think of some sort of "The dog ate my homework" excuse.

Fried Shrimp Heads
Serves 4

What an absolute exquisite treat. There are many things that chefs and accomplished cooks never let leave their kitchen. This is one of them and the reasons are many. For one, it's too damn good and we don't want to share. For two, the majority of the public would not appreciate it. Did I forget to mention that it's too damn good and we all are just greedy selfish bastards?

Selfishness is not a character flaw. Where as being completely unselfish could very well get you fired. My good buddy anonymously named "JB" was feeling the love one day. Being especially proud of his expertly tuned French technique, let a dish of some braised nutria escape his kitchen to a very enthusiastic patron. When all the bread sopping was done, the owner was informed and hence, completely aghast. Subsequently, "JB" was removed from his position. To quote my buddy "JB", "no good has ever come from sharing" or did he say "never serve nutria"? Don't know about you, I'm leaning towards the first.

Fried Shrimp Heads
The heads from one pound of 15-20 size fresh Gulf Shrimp
Cornstarch
Sea or Kosher Salt

Pre-heat your deep fryer to 360 degrees. Take the shrimp heads and break off that little spear like protrusion from the nose of the shrimp head. Toss the cornstarch all over the heads. Shake very well so that the starch coats the outside and the inside of the head. Shake off all the excess cornstarch and place the heads into the fryer. Fry until brown and crispy. Remove from the fryer on to a paper towel and season with a bit of salt. Let the heads cool slightly. This will help the shell get crispy like a chip rendering the texture more palatable. It will also let the luscious molten "fat" from the shrimp head cool so it wont take off the roof of your mouth when you bite into shellfish ecstasy. I would say serve on a lovely platter made of fine Irish Waterford Crystal. But remember, this isn't supposed to leave your kitchen. Just you and whom ever you conned into helping cook and clean. That's it!

"After Love, There is Only Cuisine"
Charlie Trotter

Crawfish Bisque
Serves 8 bowls, plus a bit extra to freeze for a rainy day.

The reason I have included this recipe in the "Head" chapter is to acknowledge and pay homage to the long lost art of stuffing the crawfish heads. In order to be a proper bisque, the heads must be stuffed and placed back into the creamy bullion. NO ONE does this anymore. I suspect laziness is the culprit and Rachel Ray, with her 30-minute meals, may very well be the catalyst. Wellllll, she may insist on making a meal in under 30 minutes at the expense of the traditions of the table. But I for one don't feel like spitting in my grandmother's face today.

Who am I kidding? Truth be told, if Oprah called me up, I would be cooking meals in 29 minutes or less! "Pasta with chicken nugget Bolognese, anyone"?

Crawfish Bisque
5 pounds live Crawfish
2 cups Sea or Kosher Salt
For the stuffing:
2 strips of finely chopped Bacon
2 Tablespoons of unsalted Butter
1/2 finely chopped Yellow Onion
1 rib of minced Celery
1/2 cup minced Green Bell Pepper
2 cloves of minced Garlic
1 Tablespoon dried Thyme
1 Tablespoon dried Oregano
1 Tablespoon dried Basil

1 teaspoon Cayenne Powder
2 cups Bread Crumbs
1 bunch of chopped Green Onions
1/2 cup chopped Italian Parsley
Sea or Kosher Salt
Flour for dusting
For the Bisque:
2 sticks of Butter
1 cup of Flour
1 chopped Yellow Onion
2 chopped ribs of Celery
1 chopped Carrot
3 cloves chopped Garlic
3 Tablespoons of Tomato Paste
1 bottle Cognac
10 sprigs of fresh Thyme
5 sprigs of fresh Tarragon
2 bay leaves
1/2 teaspoon of Cayenne Powder
Sea or Kosher Salt
freshly ground White Pepper

Place the crawfish into a colander and rinse all the mud and sand off. Place the crawfish into a large container and dump the salt into the container. Fill the container with water and let the crawfish sit for 15 minutes.

Bring a Large pot of water to a boil. When I say "large pot", use some common sense. It is to cook the 5 pounds of crawfish. So the size of vessel needed will be what ever you possess that's appropriate for the 5 pounds of crawfish you have wiggling in your large container at the moment. Strain the crawfish from the container and place the crawfish into the pot and when you see small bubbles start to rise to the surface. As the pot starts to simmer again, turn the heat off and let the crawfish sit for 5 minutes. Remove the crawfish from the pot to cool and reserve the liquid. Separate the tails from the heads. Pinch all of the tail meat out of their homes. Chop half of the meat and set aside for the stuffing. Reserve the remaining whole tails for the bisque in a separate bowl and discard the shells. Excavate all of the wonderful yellow crawfish "fat" by using your pinky finger to scoop it out of the crawfish heads. Place the "fat" on top of the reserved bisque meat. Remove any whiskers from the crawfish heads and set the heads aside.

To stuff the heads: Place the bacon and the butter into a medium sized pot over medium heat. Cook the cured pork belly until it is translucent and it has scented your kitchen with hickory. At this point add the onion and cook for 5 minutes. Then proceed to adding the celery and the bell pepper and continue to cook for another 5 minutes. Place the garlic and all of the spices and herbs into the pot and cook for one minute. Fold the breadcrumbs and the chopped crawfish from earlier into the pot and add just enough reserved crawfish stock to form a wet paste. Simmer the stuffing for another 2 minutes.

TASTE it and add any salt you feel necessary. Salt is a flavor enhancer. Treat it just like a cocktail treats your personality. Take the stuffing off of the stove and let cool.
Take your crawfish stuffing and place it into the empty heads of your crawfish friends. Don't feel bad, my friend's heads are empty too.

To make the base of the bisque: Melt the butter in a large pot over medium heat. Stir the flour into the pot and cook for 3 minutes. Cook the onion, celery and carrot in the pot for another 5 minutes. Add the garlic and tomato paste to the pot and stir while cooking for another minute. Splash in 1 cup of Cognac and be fore warned. The Cognac will likely ignite. Stand back because eyebrows are essential to equal social treatment---just ask Whoopi. Stir 3 quarts of your reserved crawfish poaching water into the pot along with the herbs and cayenne. Bring to a simmer and cook on low heat for 45 minutes. Strain the bisque through a fine mesh strainer and pour the strained liquid back into the pot. Place the stuffed crawfish heads into the pot and bring to a simmer. Pull back out the crawfish tails with the "fat" you were saving for this very instance. Place them into the pot and the second the pot starts to simmer TURN IT OFF! Taste and season again with salt and white pepper as needed.

To serve your bisque: Take the soup bowls that you so cleverly warmed in the oven and splash a 1/2 ounce of Cognac into the bottom of each one. Ladle the soup with as many stuffed heads as you see fit into the bowls. You have truly accomplished a great feat! If that doesn't make the sun of good deeds shine on you, I don't know what will.

Veal Cheeks "Sunday Pot Roast" with Madeira, Kidneys and Morels
Serves 8

I don't know about you, but my mom hardly cooked anything. My learning to become an accomplished cook is a true testament to the strength of the human will. My childhood flavor memories are filled with all-you-can eat buffets of fried catfish and chicken fried steak. Followed up with a dessert of some sort of dastardly violent Charles Bronson or Dirty Harry movie. To this day, I cannot seem to figure out which was more detrimental to my psychological well-being.

One of the 3 or 4 things my mom did have in her repertoire, along with every other matron that reads *Better Homes and Gardens*, was the Sunday Pot Roast. What can be easier than adding some stuff into a bag and popping it in the oven for a few hours?

"Sunday Pot Roast"
4 pounds Veal Cheeks
1 Veal Kidneys about a pound
2 Tablespoons of unsalted Butter
2 cups whole Pearl Onions peeled
8 whole cloves of Garlic

1 Medium Carrot peeled and cut into large circles
1 cup medium bodied Merlot
12 whole baby Red Potatoes
1 pound whole Morel Mushrooms
1 cup Celery finely chopped
1/4 cup fresh Rosemary chopped
3/4 cup Flour
2 cups Madeira
1 cup Beef Broth
4 Bay leaves
one of those oven proof Roasting Bags
Sea or Kosher Salt
Fresh cracked Black Pepper

Pre-heat your oven to 325 degrees. Trim as mush of the silver skin off of the veal cheek along with half of the fat. While you're at it and feeling confident with your blade, go ahead and trim the extra fat off of the kidney too. Pat the cheeks and kidney dry with a paper towel. Season the veal cheeks and the kidney very liberally with a heavy hand of salt and pepper. Place a large skillet over high heat and just before your fire alarm goes off add the veal cheeks. Don't crowd the pan! Just one at a time and give it a nice brown crust an all sides. Continue to treat each of your children in the same manner showing no favoritism an let them all be of equal succulence. Set the cheeks and kidney aside. While the pan is still hot, toss the onions, garlic and carrot into the pan and char them up a bit. Douse the pan with the Merlot and take maw maw's wooden spoon and scrape the bottom of the pan releasing all the intense bits and pieces of flavor nuggets. Turn off the heat and leave it be until needed.

Slice the kidney into 1/2 inch rounds and remove any veins with your knife. Place your ovenproof bag into a large casserole dish. Open the bag and layer the kidneys inside. Place the cheeks on your mattress of kidneys and place all the rest of the ingredients into the bag with a tablespoon of salt. Tie up the end of the bag and place into the oven for 3 1/2 hours.

Remove the bag from the oven and let it rest for 20 minutes. Unleash the aromas into your home by opening the bag and sliding the contents into the casserole dish. Taste the broth and add enough salt and pepper to satisfy your good judgment. Slice and serve with a crusty loaf of bread and some salted room temperature butter.

The Perfect Dinner Table

A table cloth that's slightly soiled

Where greasy little hands have toiled;

The napkins kept in silver rings,

And only ordinary things

From which to eat, a simple fare,

And just the wife and kiddies there,

And while I serve, the clatter glad

Of little girl and little lad

Who have so very much to say

About the happenings of the day.

Four big round eyes that dance with glee,

Forever flashing joys at me,

Two little tongues that race and run

To tell of troubles and of fun;

The mother with a patient smile

Who knows that she must wait awhile

Before she'll get a chance to say

What she's discovered through the day.

She steps aside for girl and lad

Who have so much to tell their dad.

Our manners may not be the best;

Perhaps our elbows often rest

Upon the table, and at times

That very worst of dinner crimes,

That very shameful act and rude

Of speaking ere you've downed your food,

Too frequently, I fear, is done,

So fast the little voices run.

Yet why should table manners stay

Those tongues that have so much to say?

At many a table I have been

Where wealth and luxury were seen,

And I have dined in halls of pride

Where all the guests were dignified;

But when it comes to pleasure rare

The perfect dinner table's where

No stranger's face is ever known:

The dinner hour we spend alone,

When little girl and little lad

Run riot telling things to dad.

Edgar Allen Guest

Moules et Oreille Frites *Steamed Mussels with Pig Ear Fries*
Serves 4 Family Style

My love for seafood and pork is no big secret. My lineage is purely South Louisiana, where both the swine and the seafood rule the kingdom. Even though the mussels are not a native mollusk to my heritage, my foundation serenades me into adding add pork in one fashion or another to almost every seafood dish. The classical *Moules Frites* plate calls for French fries. I have taken the artistic freedom to substitute crispy pig ears for the fries. If I could gorge my face everyday with French fries I most certainly would! But the crackle and gelatinous toothsome bite of the ears brings this dish to a new level.

Moules et Oreille Frites
3 Pig ears
1 Yellow Onion peeled and chopped
2 stalks of Celery chopped
1 Carrot peeled and chopped
4 Cloves of Garlic
2 Bay leaves
1 tablespoon whole Black Peppercorns
5 sprigs of fresh Thyme
3 tablespoons Creole Mustard
2 cups flour
1 egg
1 cup of milk
2 cups of breadcrumbs
1 tablespoon dried Thyme
2 tablespoons Olive Oil
1 cup diced Andouille Sausage
2 Shallots peeled and sliced
3 cloves of Garlic sliced
2 teaspoons Red Pepper Flakes
2 quarts Mussels scrubbed and debearded
1 1/2 cups crisp White Wine
5 tablespoons of unsalted Butter
10 basil leaves
1/2 cup Italian Parsley roughly chopped
1 whole Lemon
Sea or Kosher Salt and freshly cracked black pepper

Take one of your favorite medium sized pots and place the Ears, onions, celery, carrot, garlic, bay leaves, peppercorns and thyme in it. Pour in 2 quarts of water with a tablespoon of salt. Bring the pot to a simmer and cook on a very low heat for 3 hours. Remove the ears from the liquid and let cool. Strain the liquid and save for a rainy day with some forgiving beans perhaps.

Cut the ears into ½-inch batons. Place the ear batons into a bowl and dress them up with the mustard. Place the flour in a separate bowl and toss in a tablespoon of salt. Crack the eggs and whisk in the milk in yet another bowl. Finally, add the breadcrumbs, dried thyme and a tablespoon of salt into, that's right, another bowl. Dredge the ears into the flour, then into the egg wash, then into the breadcrumbs. Hold them in the breadcrumbs and pre-heat your deep fryer to 360 degrees.

Get out a large pot to which you are still in possession of the lid. Place the pot on high heat and drizzle in the olive oil. When the oil begins to get upset and smoke, add the andouille and shallots. Cook for 2 minutes or until the shallots start to brown ever so lightly. Put the garlic slices and the red pepper in and cook for 1 minute. Stir often to keep your guests from burning. Add the mussels to the pot and toss everything together with a few good stirs from a large spoon. Douse the pot with the wine and butter then snuggle the lid on to the top of the pot. Steam the mussels for 4 minutes or until they open. You may have one or two uncooperative mussels that don't want to open up and be a part of the discussion. Discard any that don't open.

Pour the contents of the whole pot into a large serving bowl. Sift your pig ears out of the breadcrumbs and place into the fryer. While you are listening to the ears, they should be listening to you as you squeeze the juice of the whole lemon over the bowl of mussels and you tear the basil with your hands. Let your hands use God as a little guidance and rain the herbs all over the mussels. Pull the golden brown crispy ear frites out of the fryer and mound them over the top of the mussels.
Place the bowl on a decent size bar table or counter. Pull out a loaf of bread and 4 bottles of wine. Make everyone stand, eat and tear bread with a touch of incivility.

Hog Head Egg Benedict
Serves 4

I was once asked to cite my culinary philosophy. "Anything is better fried or with a runny egg" was my response. I created this dish for some executives of the Disney Corporation. They were scouring the country for some decent chefs to help host their annual World of Food and Wine event and they just so happened upon my kitchen. Desperately wanting a free trip to see my pant-less buddy Donald with his ever so curious speech impediment. I decided to tip the scales in my favor and create something that starred both ends of my philosophy. It was a wonderful October indeed.

Hogs Head Egg Benedict
For the biscuits:
1 1/2 cups Flour plus a little extra for dusting
2 teaspoons Kosher or Sea Salt
1 tablespoon Sugar

1 tablespoon Baking Powder
1 stick of unsalted Butter, cubed
1/2 cup Milk
For the Bearnaise:
1 bottle crisp White Wine
2 Tablespoons fresh Tarragon
1 bottle Tabasco
3 Egg Yolks
2 cups warm Clarified Butter
For the Benedict:
8 4x4 inch slices of Hog Head Cheese, cut 3/4 an inch thick
2 cups Flour
9 Eggs
1 cup Milk
2 teaspoons cream of tartar or 1 ounce vinegar
Sea or Kosher Salt
chopped Green Onion to garnish

To Bake the Biscuits:

Pre-heat your oven to 400 degrees. Marry the flour, salt, sugar and baking powder together in a mixing bowl. Plop the butter into the flour and use your fingers to dismantle the butter in the flour until the butter cubes have been reduced to peas. Form a well in the center of the flour and pour in the milk. Gently pull together all of the ingredients until a dough forms. The dough should be slightly sticky and damp. If the dough is too wet to handle as one uniform mass, add a little more flour to pull it together. Powder a section of your counter with some flour and place the biscuit dough on top. Apply a little flour to the top of your dough and flatten the dough with your hands until it is 1 inch in uniform thickness. Cut the dough into 6 biscuits. Arrange the biscuits on a baking pan so that their shoulders are touching side by side. Bake those little soldiers in the oven for 20 minutes. Take out and let cool.

For the Bearnaise:

In the smallest of pans, pour in 2 cups of white wine with 4 dashes of Tabasco and the tarragon. Bring to a simmer and reduce the liquid until there is scantly enough to call a shot. Set aside to cool.

Fill a medium sized bowl with a few inches of water and place it on the stove over a medium heat. Take one of your trusty stainless steel bowls and place the egg yolks, 1 ounce of wine and 3 dashes of Tabasco into the trusted vessel. Whisk the goodies together and place the bowl on top the pot of water. Start whisking over the steaming mad pot until the mixture is very thick and doubled in volume. This will take a determined tri-cep and a will as steadfast as a radical feminist. But your reward in the end will be boundless. Remove the thickened silky ribbon of egg yolks and stir in your wine reduction. Taste it and add some salt accordingly. Set aside in a place no warmer than your laundry room and no colder than your mother-in-law's disposition.

To Assemble the Benedict:

Pre-heat your fryer to 360 degrees. Place 2 quarts of water with 1 tablespoon of salt and the cream of tartar into a medium sized pot and bring the pot to a simmer on top of the stove. Put the flour into a bowl with 1 tablespoon of salt. In a separate bowl, whisk together 1 egg and the milk. Dust each slice of headcheese with flour. Then dip into the egg wash then back into the flour they go. Set on a plate or leave in the flour until you are ready in a few minutes. Lay out your 4 plates. Cut the biscuits horizontally into halves and place 2 of the halves with their cut side exposed to the sky on each plate. Crack the eggs carefully into the simmering water. While the eggs are poaching, fry the 8 slices of headcheese until they are crispy and golden. Remove from the fryer and place one slice on each biscuit half. Use a large slotted spoon and remove each egg from the water. Wrap a towel around your hand as if you were getting ready to punch the window of a lover who did you wrong and gently tilt the spoon into your wrapped hand so the towel will absorb any excess water. Place the egg on top of one of the fried headcheese slices and do the same for the next 7 eggs. Don't hesitate or the personality of your eggs will stiffen. No one wants to be friends with an egg whose yolk doesn't ooze with charm. Drape a few heaping spoonfuls of the béarnaise over each egg and scatter some green onion over that. Serve to your friends, perhaps with the D'Artagnan and brined Bacon from the first chapter for a truly glorious start to any morning---especially a Tuesday.

"Some people say less is more. Well, it's not. More is More."
Me

Tongue and Gravy Deep Fried Po Boy
Serves 4

Growing up in New Orleans has more advantages than disadvantages. Your taught an appreciation for fine foodways at a very early age. I remember going to City Park and eating Roast Beef Po Boys. The warm gravy and beef would mix with the chill of the mayo, tomato and crisp lettuce to form a lush nectar that would literally run down your arm as it succumbed from the weight of your bite into the crackling and chewy French bread. It was instilled in me at the age of 8, that if the gravy didn't run down your arm, it wasn't a properly dressed Po Boy. Thanks to the Po Boy, I haven't been properly dressed since.

Tongue and Gravy Deep Fried Po Boy
1 Beef Tongue about 2.5 pounds
1 Yellow Onion peeled and roughly chopped
2 stalks of Celery roughly chopped
8 cloves of Garlic

1 medium Carrot roughly chopped
2 Bay Leaves
2 teaspoons of freshly ground Black Pepper
8 sprigs of fresh Thyme
1 quart of Beef Broth
1/3 cup Butter
1/3 cup Flour
1 loaf New Orleans French Bread
Mayonnaise
shredded Iceberg lettuce
slices of Tomato
slices of pickle
Sea or Kosher Salt
For the Frying Batter:
2 cups Flour
2 teaspoons Baking Powder
1 teaspoon Sea or Kosher Salt
1 Egg
2 cups Milk

Get a medium sized braising pot with a nice fitting lid out of one of your cabinets. Put the tongue, onion, celery, garlic, carrot, bay leaves, pepper, thyme and beef broth into your pot. Bring the pot to a simmer over medium-high heat. Cover your tongue with the lid and lower the heat to very low. Let the tongue bathe in the broth for 1 hour and 10 minutes. Uncover the pot, turn off the heat and let the tongue ponder life in the pot for 20 minutes. Remove the tongue and set aside. Strain the stock into a container and place the pot back onto the stove. Melt the butter over low heat and stir in the flour until they are unified and agreeable to the task at hand. Pour the strained broth into the roux and let the mixture simmer for a few minutes. Turn off the heat, taste the gravy and season it with salt and pepper to your delight. Trim, peel and discard the outer tough layer of the tongue. Slice the tongue thinly and place it into the gravy. Hold aside and keep warm with love and attention.

For the Frying Batter:
Mix all the ingredients together in a bowl and hold aside until someone screams "Show Time".

To Assemble the Po Boys:
Pre-heat your fryer to 375 degrees. Cut the French bread into quarters. Then cut each quarter horizontally 3/4 of the way through, so that it will open like a clamshell. Spread an enjoyable amount of mayonnaise on the inside of the 4 sandwiches. Divide the sliced Tongue amongst the sandwiches equally or unequally; it is up to you how you want to treat your friends. Place the lettuce, tomato and pickle into the Po Boys. Close the "clam shell" up and insert 2 toothpicks into the lips of each Po Boy to keep their mouth closed while in the fryer. Have someone loudly proclaim "SHOW TIME". Then dip each Po Boy into the batter and dip the Po Boy so slowly into the fryer that it is literally starting to fry

while still in your hand. This will help the Po Boy not to stick to your fryer basket. Just watch what you are doing and try not to be too inebriated to the point of burning yourself like an idiot. Fry God's favorite sandwich on both sides until golden in your fryer.
Take it out and repeat for everyone else. Cut each one into two and smother it in what you call Gravy but I prefer to say Amber Justice.

Tongue Daube Glace
Serves 10

Daube is a classic Creole beef stew. Daube Glace is the same stew chilled and jellied into a mold. Then you slice a piece or two and enjoy atop some French bread or a cracker. In my version I have exchanged the beef for beef tongue. Once as a deviant joke, I used the tongue with some pork "fries" in the glace. Just think about that for a moment.
If you can't start a party with some meat jello, maybe you need a flock of new companions.

Tongue Daube Glace
1 quart Water
1 cup sugar
1/2 cup Sea or Kosher Salt
1 tablespoon Fennel seeds
1 teaspoon Red Pepper Flakes
2 Tablespoons Creole Mustard
1 tablespoon dried Oregano
2 tablespoons minced fresh Garlic
4 Bay leaves
1 tablespoon Celery Seed
1 Beef Tongue
1 1/2 cups red wine
1/2 Yellow Onion minced
1 stalk of Celery minced
1 cup Carrot minced
1/2 cup Italian Parsley chopped
1/2 ounce of powdered Gelatin

Retrieve a medium sized pot and place into the pot the 1 quart of water, sugar, salt, fennel, red pepper, mustard, oregano, garlic, bay leaves and celery seed. Bring the mixture to a simmer and stir until the sugar and salt have dissolved. Set the liquid brine into the cooler to completely chill. Then drown the tongue in your brine. Please resist the little devil on your shoulder that is telling you to rub the tongue on the back of a mate's unsuspecting ear. NOTHING good will come of this! Place a plate on top of the tongue to hold it below the surface of the brine. Allow the tongue to live in the brine for 2 days. Take the seasoned tongue out of the cooler and remove the plate that was keeping the brine submerged. Add 2 cups of water to the pot that is accommodating your tongue and brine. Place the pot onto the stove and bring to a simmer. Cover the pot with something useful like a lid. Simmer the tongue slowly for 1 hour and 10 minutes. Turn off the heat, remove the lid and let the tongue cool in the pot for 30 minutes. Remove the tongue and trim off the outer tough layer. Dice the tongue into 1/2 inch cubes and save for later. Pull another pot out of your cabinet and to it add 2 cups of the brine, the red wine, onion, celery and carrot. Bring to a simmer over low heat and cook for 15 minutes. Turn off the heat, stir in the diced tongue and the parsley. Add the gelatin as directed by the respected manufacturer. Pour the jello into a mold and place in your cooler over night to stiffen. Once your tongue jello is set, un-mold with a flair of revelry for your friends to admire then enjoy.

Fried Green Tomato GLT
Serves 4

The BLT is the classic American sandwich. I haven't run across one recipe that wasn't screaming for a little slap and tickle of Southern refinement. Hence the fried green tomatoes and the guanciale. Guanciale is a pork jowl that has been cured but not smoked. It is a great substitution for bacon in the sandwich. It is as equally delightful if you crisp a few cubes to keep in your pocket and pop in your mouth to keep your spirits high and your breath desirable.

Fried Green Tomato GLT
8 slices of Rye sandwich bread
16 slices of Guanciale
8 slices of Green Tomato
2 cups Flour
1 Egg
1 cup Milk
2 cups Breadcrumbs
1 tablespoon dried Thyme
1 head of Butter Lettuce
Sea or Kosher Salt
freshly ground Black Pepper
For the Horseradish Dressing:
2 cups Mayonnaise
3/4 cup Milk
1/2 cup Red Onion minced
1/2 cup Green Onion chopped
2 cloves of Garlic minced
1 cup Horseradish
1 tablespoon dried Oregano
1 tablespoon dried Thyme
1 tablespoon dried Basil

Pre-heat your oven to 375 degrees. Lay the strips of guanciale on a baking tray and cook in the oven until crisp. Take the crispy jowls off of the pan and pat dry with a paper towel. Hold aside the guanciale and try not to eat any unless you don't mind shorting one or two or five of your guests.

Pre-heat your deep fryer to 360 degrees. Put the flour with one tablespoon of salt into a bowl and mix it. Whisk together the egg and milk in a separate bowl. Finally, into the last available bowl you have clean, place the breadcrumbs in it with the thyme and one tablespoon of salt and pepper. Stir to combine. Dredge each slice of tomato into the flour then dip into the egg wash and then flop the into the breadcrumbs making sure it is coated quite well. Place the breaded tomatoes on a plate or leave them in the breadcrumbs until they are queued for the finale.

For the Horseradish Dressing:
Mix all the ingredients together. You can make this well in advance. Be careful to save some for the sandwich. It all might disappear the next time you grill some ox heart. Assemble the Sandwich:
Insert the bread into the toaster and cook. Start frying the green tomatoes. Cook them until they are crispy and brown. Take them out of the fryer and pat dry on a paper towel. Lather the toast with horseradish dressing. Lay 2 slices of fried tomato on 4 pieces of the toast. Drape a few leaves of lettuce over the top of the tomatoes. Then lay 4 slices of guanciale on top of that. Place the 4 lonely pieces of toast on top of the sandwiches. Cut the sandwiches in halves and serve them to your lunch friends. I suspect the succotash salad in the last chapter would be a great companion to the sandwich.

"With the Genius Comes the Madness"
Me

Cervelles De Veau Beignets with Sauce Ravigote
Serves 4

Every restaurant has a way to dupe the public and in the process make more money. One way is to call things by their French name. Braised Chicken $12 or Coq Au Vin $20. Pork and Beans $8 or Cassoulet $22. It is also a clever way to fool your guests into eating something they might not try on a normal basis. Would you care for some petite fried nuggets of Cervelles de Veau? Sounds delightfully delicious. "I'll have 2, Thank You sir". Or it could be, fried brain McNuggets? "I'll take my bottle of young undrinkable Cabernet back and I'm leaving now" will be the inevitable response.

Cervelles de Veau Beignets with Sauce Ravigote
For the Sauce Ravigote:
1 cup Mayonnaise

1/2 cup Creole Mustard
1 tablespoon Capers
3 dashes of Tabasco
2 teaspoons horseradish
1 boiled Egg chopped
1/3 cup Green Onion chopped
1/2 Lemon juiced
For the Beignets:
2 Calves Brains about 12 ounces each
1/2 cup crisp White Wine
1 Shallot chopped
2 cloves of Garlic chopped
1 tablespoon dried Tarragon
For the Batter:
1 cup Flour
1 teaspoon baking powder
2 egg whites
Sea or Kosher Salt

For the Ravigote sauce:
Mix all the ingredients together and set aside in your cooler. This can easily be made a day or so in advance if your bored and have nothing to do for 5 minutes.

For the Beignets:
Place the brains in a container larger than the original container and cover with water. Add a small handful of salt and refrigerate over night. Remove the brains and rinse them. Then place them in a pot and cover with water. Place the pot on your best burner and turn the heat as high as your loftiest aspirations. The moment the water starts to simmer, pour the brains out into a colander. Rinse for a couple of minutes with some cold water and gently place them in your refrigerator for 1 hour. Reach behind all the Champagne in your refrigerator and pull the chilled brains back out. Remove any membrane and veins you might see. Then slice the brain into 1/3 inch slices. Place the slices into a bowl and add the wine, shallot, garlic and tarragon. Slightly mix the ingredients up a bit and let the brains marinate for 4 to 6 hours. "Brain marinating in wine for 4 to 6 hours?" Sounds like a good plan to me!

For the Batter:
Place the flour, baking powder and a pinch of salt into a decent size bowl. Very slowly whisk in 1 cup of water so that there are no lumps and the batter is smooth. Cover with wrap, marinate your brain with some more wine and leave the batter alone for 2 hours. In a separate bowl, whisk the egg whites until the peaks of the whites are stiff and stand attention as they point to the sky. Fold the egg whites into the flour batter until all is light and fluffy and smooth.

To Assemble:

Pre-heat your deep fryer to 360 degrees. Remove the brain slices from the marinade and pat dry. Dip the slices into the batter and fry for a few minutes until each side is golden brown. Remove from the fryer and drain on a paper towel. Season with some salt. Serve the Cervelle with the Ravigote sauce and for the love of God, DONT SAY "BRAINS".

Chapter 3: NECK

The Significance of Bread

There has never been a more versatile ingredient in your pantry than bread. It has helped the primitive man sustain life as well as enriching the noble man's life for centuries. Bread is widely perceived just as an accompaniment to most meals. But when was the last time someone you valued proclaimed, "Lets break truffles together"? You should put just as much thought into how and what kinds of breads you serve as any conductor would his horn section.

Bread is similar to salt in the significance of the table. It will not only enhance a meal beyond mundane, but it will bind the parts of a few well thought out ingredients into a whole. It aids in binding the camaraderie of the family at the table. A meal served without bread is a definitive confirmation of one's lack of regard for sustaining the life of the family. Also in sustaining the life of his social worth.

I never throw bread away. Granted, I don't let it turn into a furry blue Cha Cha Cha Chia Pet. But at the end of every meal, I will wrap and freeze any left over bread that hasn't been drooled on by the guest that was brought by another guest. Left over bread is the staple of many country's diets. Here in America, the land where wasteful attitudes is an assumed birthright, we don't hesitate to throw out the foundation of some of the world's greatest dishes right along with our morality. Perhaps that attitude is cultivated by the fact that restaurants give you so much of it for "free". If it is "free" and it is everywhere, then surely it must be OK to discard it with the bones of the fried chicken. The next time you buy a $4 glass of iced tea or an $8 Iceberg salad, sit and ponder just how "free" your bread has become.

Some wonderful uses for old bread are:

Meatballs. No great meatball was ever made with packaged Italian breadcrumbs. You must take cubed day old bread and soak it in milk. Then squeeze out the milk and use that to bind the meatballs. Meatballs are actually mostly bread in Italy. But what do they know?

Crumble bread into large coarse crumbs and fry in a skillet with some olive oil. You can use this to garnish risotto, beans, soups or anything that has a soft character. Contrasting textures are key in keeping the palate excited and your chances of love high.

Crostini for cheese. I will take the left over loaves and cut them into crostini. Brush with olive oil and bake in the oven until lightly brown. Upon removal from the oven I may be inclined to rub the crostini with a raw clove of garlic. That depends on how I'm feeling at the moment. Pile them up next to the cheese board and let everyone have at it. Bread is for cheese, crackers are for church.

Bread Pudding. What an utterly simple yet refined dessert that absolutely anyone with a touch of decent sense can create. After all, it's just eggs, milk, sugar and old bread. Just be sure to have the whiskey sauce too. Nothing highlights the end of an evening like the warm sweet kiss of Kentucky.

My personal governing laws on how to properly use bread are fairly simple:

Bread should never be sliced into individual servings. How are you ever supposed to make that eternal bond at the table with your guests if you literally do not "break bread" together?

Using the same thought process that you administer to pair wine with food, you use to pair bread with food. Should the bread be sour to heighten the flavor of the fish? Should the bread be dark and rich for the roasted lamb? Just fall back on the flavors that you can recall in your mind and match the bread to help consummate the union.

Toasting or grilling of bread should never be done ahead of time. The bread is full of fresh personality when it has just exited the grill to be splashed with a perfume of olive oil and a sprinkling of herbs. It's warm, moist, soft soul and crisp exterior presents the same allure as that of a beautiful woman with naughty tendencies.

My whole goal through this volume of cookery is to have you step back and take all the facets of dining you are providing into equal consideration. All the Baccarat, D'quem and caviar in the world couldn't save the demise of your evening when you allow prejudice to infiltrate the importance of the humble service of bread.

Veal Neck Braciola
Serves 8

Braciola is a classic Italian recipe for stuffing and braising a piece of meat then serving it with "Red Gravy". The rest of the world may call it "marinara" but I'm from the Westbank of New Orleans and we call it "Red Gravy". In my first year of attendance at the New England Culinary Institute we were at the start of service and I threw a question out to the instructor, "Where on the plate to you want me to put the Red Gravy?". "We do not serve **Gravy** here David, we serve Sauce".

I have used many different things to make Braciola from the classic pork loin to chicken thighs. In my effort to make sure no prejudice is shown towards any portion of the animal, I created this recipe.

Veal Neck Braciola
1/2 Veal Neck boned
For the Stuffing:
Extra Virgin Olive Oil
1 Yellow Onion minced
2 stalks of Celery minced
4 cloves of Garlic minced
1 cup diced Andouille sausage
1 cup fresh Breadcrumbs
1/2 cup Italian Parsley chopped

1 Tablespoon fresh Thyme leaves
1/2 cup of Golden Raisins
2 teaspoons Red Pepper Flakes
1/2 cup grated Parmesan Cheese
5 boiled Eggs
Sea or Kosher Salt
freshly ground Black Pepper

For the Braising Sauce:
1 Yellow Onion minced
2 stalks of Celery minced
1 Green Bell Pepper minced
4 cloves of Garlic minced
1 tablespoon dried Oregano
2 Bay leaves
1 cup White Wine
1 28oz can of Tomato Puree
1 28oz can of Whole peeled Italian Plum Tomatoes

For the Garnish:
1 orange
1/3 cup Pine Nuts toasted
1/2 cup of fresh chopped herbs such as Basil, Oregano, Thyme and Parsley

For the Stuffing:
Place a large pot over medium heat and drizzle in 2 tablespoons of olive oil. Saute the onion for 3 minutes seasoning with a dash of salt just as any cook with good sense. Add the celery and continue to cook for another 5 minutes. Stir in the garlic and let the aroma bellow from the pot making you hungry for another minute. Take the pot off of the heat and place the cooked contents in a medium sized mixing bowl. Take your andouille, breadcrumbs, parsley, thyme, raisins, red pepper flakes and parmesan and add it to the bowl. Mix the stuffing up and set it aside. Go ahead and set the large pot back aside to use later.

Take your boned veal neck and pound it with confidence until it is about 1/2-1/3 inch flat. Season both sides of the veal with a liberal amount of salt and pepper. Lay your veal neck flat and evenly distribute the stuffing that you have reserved in the bowl across the surface of the veal. Place the boiled eggs end to end horizontally across the first 1/3rd portion of the veal. Roll the veal over the eggs and continue to roll forming a pinwheel. Take some butchers twine and tie the pinwheel up. You want the pinwheel to be as snug and comfortable as you might feel on a third date. So don't tie the veal too tight or you will loose your eggs during the cooking process along with your new romance.

For the Braising Sauce:
Pre-heat your oven to 325 degrees. Place the large pot from earlier back onto the stove over high heat. Splatter in 1 tablespoon of olive oil and wait for it to get angry and start

smoking. Lay your veal pinwheel into the pot and brown it. Be careful not to fiddle with the meat until it is clearly browned and ready to be turned. Once the meat is perfectly browned all over, take it out of the pot and set it aside on a tray. Add the onion to the hot pot. Sprinkle a touch of salt over the onion, because all proper cooks season things as they go and cook while stirring for 2 minutes. Place the celery and bell pepper into the pot and cook for another 5 minutes. Put the garlic, dried oregano and bay leaves into the pot and once again let the aroma bellow into the kitchen for 1 minute. Add the wine and tomato puree to the pot. Then using your hands, squeeze the canned whole tomatoes to break them up and also place them into the pot. Put the veal braciola into your pot and bring it all to a happy simmer. Cover the pot with a lid and place into your oven for one hour. Remove the lid from the pot and raise the oven's temperature to 375 degrees. Cook for an additional 20 minutes.

Take the pot out of the stove and let the meat rest in all of the sauce for 20 minutes. Remove the braciola from the pot and snip the twine from the meat. Pour a fair amount of sauce onto a large serving platter. Slice the braciola into 1 inch thick slices and place on the platter. Zest the orange over the braciola and sprinkle with the pine nuts and which ever herbs you have chosen with your experienced palate. To really be the envy of the block you should highly consider serving this with Grits a la Wop. After all, jealousy is a sure sign of utmost success.

Tuna Collar in Purgatory
Serves 2

It is impossible for one day to follow another without a fight of good and evil within the soul. Those two little guys pop up one one's shoulder and battle it out for your morality. Since the edicts of morality are self-governing, I am proud to announce that Good triumphs in every single instance in my life. In my own self-perceived lenient view, the two little guys on my shoulder are both of the same cloth. I just happen to be sporadically color blind out of convenience.

This dish represents the same battle. The good of God's collar swimming amongst the spicy flames of Lucifer's chiles. From the way they taste together, you are forced to question if they could actually exist without each other?

Tuna Collar in Purgatory
1 pound of Tuna Collar cut into manageable pieces
Sea or Kosher Salt
5 Ancho Chiles seeded and stemmed
1/3 cup toasted Almonds
3/4 cup extra virgin Olive Oil
2 cups canned whole Italian Plum Tomatoes

2 cloves of Garlic
1 teaspoon Red Pepper flakes
2 tablespoons of Rice Vinegar
8 small fingerling or baby yukon gold Potatoes
chopped fresh Italian Parsley
1/2 lemon for juicing

Fill a medium sized pot with water and season the water with salt until you are reminded of the childhood summers spent at the sea. Place the potatoes into the pot and put your pot onto the stove over medium high heat. Simmer the potatoes until their tenderness can only be seen by their willingness to accept the piercing of a sharp knife. Relieve the potatoes from their bath and let them cool on the counter.

Take the tuna collar pieces and spread the kindness of your salt over the fish. Let the fish sit for 5 minutes. Place the fish into the same pot and fill until the water covers the fish. Bring to a simmer and cook the fish for 5 minutes. Remove the pot from the heat and add the ancho chiles to the pot. Let the tuna and chiles cool in the water. Puree the chiles, almonds, olive oil, tomatoes, garlic, red pepper flakes and vinegar by whatever means you have available. Taste your purgatory puree and make sure there is enough of the devil present. Add any more salt or red pepper flakes as needed to really feel like you have sinned.

Pre-heat the oven to the high broiler mode. Place the potatoes one at a time on your cutting board and slightly smash them with the bottom of a pot or the palm of your hand just until their jackets open and flash you a bit of their flesh. Toss the potatoes with the purgatory sauce and pour it all into a large casserole dish. Drizzle a little extra olive oil on the tuna and mount the tuna with the skin shinning towards the heavens on top of the potato mixture. Nestle the tuna slightly down into the sauce leaving the skin unencumbered by a blanket of sin and free to crispin. Place the casserole into the oven on the middle rack and cook for 20 minutes. Remove the dish from your oven. Sprinkle parsley and the lemon juice over the dish and serve to your lover. I suggest chopsticks for your implement of choice. They are better suited for the task of extracting the meat from the bone.

As you dine with your lover you must remember that good and evil are only what you personally perceive it to be.

Food is akin to currency. It is neither inherently moral or immoral, it's what we do with it that makes it that way.
Me

Fried Snapper Necks
Serves 2

The true delicacies of any dining establishment can only be found around midnight. As the song of the dining patrons fade and the hum of the kitchen is reduced to a few scattered mumblings of the last pot being freed of its work load. The staff gets to partake in the same pleasures of the table that have taunted them all night long. This time is called "Family Meal". This is when I go to eat.

Family Meal may be comprised of ingredients that appear to be meager in cost but I assure you, they are superior in flavor. These are all the elements that the kitchen has been hoarding for themselves. Why waste the time to cook such "poor man's" food to an unappreciative public. Give the bland and pointless Filet Mignon to them. Save the flank, the shank and the collars for us.

The first time I had fried snapper necks was at the Family Meal of a Chinese restaurant called the Lucky Palace. Yes, some may call it crashing. I figure the currier obviously kept my invitation for his own black market needs. The fried necks reminded me of great fried chicken, juice bursting along with each bite near the bone. This really could not possibly get any simpler.

Fried Snapper Necks
The neck of 2, 5-6 pound Red Snappers cut into pieces
Louisiana hot sauce
2 cups corn flour
1/2 cup corn meal
Creole blackening seasoning
Sea or Kosher Salt
2 Eggs
2 cups Milk
Lemons and buttery sweet yeast Buns to garnish

Place the snapper neck pieces into a bowl. Liberally douse them with some thick red random Louisiana hot sauce. It is my feeling that Tabasco is a bit too much for this application. Set the fish aside to mingle with the hot sauce for 30 to 60 minutes. In the mean time, pre-heat your deep fryer to 360 degrees. In one bowl, mix together the corn flour, corn meal and the blackening seasoning to taste. If you like your fried fish to draw a sweat on your brow, add generous amount of blackening seasoning. If you enjoy it as mild as an November morning, add less seasoning and more salt. Whichever path you choose, you still must season the flour and taste it to be certain there is enough flavor to recall the ocean upon your tongue. In a second bowl, whisk together the eggs and milk. Take the snapper necks and toss them into the flour mixture. Then let them swim in the egg wash. Send them for a final dusting of flour and gently drop them into the fryer. Fry the necks until golden and they are starting to come up for air. Scatter the fried necks on some paper towels with some wedges of lemon and some buttery sweet rolls. Be prepared to cleanse your finger tips with your mouth. These necks are truly finger licking good!

Smoked Pork Neck with White Beans
Serves 4

It is in good manners and faith, that on Monday's, all the kitchens of New Orleans are filled with the simmering pots of red kidney beans, sausage, rice and laundry. The tale states that the Creole slaves would cook red beans and rice on Mondays due to the ease of letting the cauldron toil while the week's dirty laundry was attended to.

Nothing exemplifies the spirit of a peasant turned king like a pot of perfectly cooked beans. My heart holds such an endearing place for the dish, that I take my home tradition one step further by cooking any kind of bean on Monday. But I digress when it comes to the laundry and wisely leave it to the professionals.

Smoked Pork Neck with White Beans
1lb heirloom Cannellini beans such as Rancho Gordo
2 tablespoons of Olive Oil
1 yellow Onion minced
2 stalks of Celery minced
1 medium Carrot peeled and minced
5 cloves of Garlic minced
2 Bay leaves
1 1/2 lbs of smoked Pork Neck
Pork or Chicken stock or even water if you are desperate
coarse kosher or sea Salt
1 bunch of Kale stemmed and cut into strips
10 Sage leaves shredded
Pecorino Romano
real green extra virgin Olive Oil
Crusty Artisan Bread

Take a large container from your pantry and let the beans fall into the bowl like the rain on a tin roof. Fill your bean container with water until it doubles the volume of the beans. Let the beans soak in the water overnight. Place the olive oil into an appropriate size pot, in which you have a lid, and place your good judgment over a stove that you have adjusted the burner to a medium-low heat. Once the pot is hot and the oil is dancing, add the onion and cover the pot with a tight fitting lid. Cook the onion for 5 minutes all the while giving it a good stir every minute or so. After cooking the onion clear for 5 minutes, add the celery and carrot to the pot and recover your vessel. Cook and stir for an additional 5 minutes before adding the garlic and bay leaves to the pot. Once again, cook for an additional minute. Lay your pork neck pieces into the pot and strain the beans from the soaking water. Add the beans to the pot along with enough stock to cover the "Pork and Beans" by 3 inches. Raise the volume of your flame to high and bring the pot to a simmer. Once the pot is simmering, replace the lid and turn your flame's volume back down to low. Let your Pork and Beans frolic in the pot for 3 hours and 10 minutes. I like the density of the bean to appear slightly more yielding than I imagine my desires to be. The beans will firm up slightly upon serving just like your morals.

Take the lid off of the pot liberating the aroma into your presence. Taste the pot's liquor and add the suitable amount of salt. Shuffle the Kale into the pot and cover again for 10 more minutes. Turn off the volume of the flame and place the sage into the pot. Cover the pot and let your ingredients get acquainted for 10 minutes. Since life is too short to eat with people you don't care for, lay out 4 large warm bowls. Place a husky toasted slice of bread into the bowl and ladle your pork and beans over the bread. Upon acceptance of your friends, drizzle that great olive oil you've been saving over the top of the Pork and Beans. Use your vegetable peeler and ribbon a little of the cheese over that lily too.

"Simplicity has no cloak for a lack of excellence"
Me

Sweetbread Spiedini with Anchovy Bagna Cauda
Serves 4

Spiedini is the Italian moniker for "meat on a stick" while Bagna Cauda is the term for "hot bath". One of your primary goals as a fine host is to evoke fond childhood memories. We will always hold dear to our hearts the times we spent as an adolescent at the Carnival. The thrilling coasters, decrepit carnies, oversize stuffed purple gorillas and of coarse, fried meat on a stick. My recipe that follows, helps you take your guests by the hand and bring them back to the days of no cares. A comforting portion of fried meat on a stick along with a heavy hand of Prosecco has me wanting to spend a week's pay trying to win that goldfish all over again.

Although, the less than fond "hot bath" was just an obstruction in the way of watching a sensational episode of *Charlie's Angeles*. Farrah Fawcett had the feathered hair of 20 angels!

Sweetbread Spiedini with Anchovy Bagna Cauda
1 pound Veal Sweetbreads
1/4 cup Rice Wine Vinegar
1/3 cup extra virgin Olive Oil
6 minced Anchovies
4 cloves of minced Garlic
2 tablespoons of unsalted Butter
1 tablespoon minced Capers
1/2 cup chopped Italian Parsley
1/2 Lemon
1 pound fresh Mozzarella
1/2 loaf of crusty artisan Bread
8 wooden skewers about 6 inches in length

4 Eggs
Kosher or Sea Salt to use as needed

Put the beautiful pink sweetbreads into a pot. Add the vinegar into the vessel and cover the gland with water. Add a tablespoon or so of salt, however much that will leave you confident that you have treated this animal with proper respect. Bring the pot to a simmer and turn off the heat. Cover the pot and let the sweetbread soak in the hot bath for 5 minutes. If you are feeling very steadfast of tackling this task in a most professional manner, take the sweetbreads out of its bath and place them into a bowl filled with ice water for 10 minutes. If you are saving your ice for the Prosecco bucket, take your sweetbreads out of their bath and just put them on a plate. Then into the refrigerator they must go to cool.

For the Bagna Cauda: Place the olive oil and anchovies into a small pot and lay over a low flame. Let the oil slowly disintegrate the anchovies for about 5 minutes. Add the garlic to the pot and cook for an additional 2 minutes. Place your butter, capers and parsley into the pot. Give your pot a few swirls and squeeze in the juice of that half of a lemon you have on the counter. Hold the "hot bath" aside in the pot for later.

For the Spiedini: Retrieve the sweetbreads from the refrigerator and remove any visible veins or membrane that may be on the gland. Cut your sweetbread into 16 pieces reminiscent of a nugget or cube. Take the mozzarella and cube it too into 16 pieces. Now present the loaf of bread to your cutting board and cut 16 similar size cubes of bread. Impale each wooden skewer with a sweetbread nugget then a piece of cheese then a piece of bread until you have all 8 spears filled with 2 pieces of each the gland, cheese and bread.

Pre-heat your fryer to 350 degrees. Get your hot bath warm by placing the Bagna Cauda over a low heat. Crack the 4 eggs into a bowl and whisk them vigorously until they are well mixed and frothy. Coat each one of your skewers into the egg and then fry until golden on each side. Remove the Spiedini from the fryer and lay on a plate. Pour the Bagna Cauda into a bowl wide enough to allow those dirty Spiedini to be bathed. Serve them to your friends with a little Prosecco and a lot of childhood enthusiasm.

Chapter 4: Torso

The Significance of Stock

As respectable and even disrespect-able human beings, we are always in search for the greater meaning to it all. The superficial and easy to read exterior answers are fine for some who display identical character flaws. But for crusaders of truth, we must look deeper. It is only after you strip back the layers of modern prejudices will you find the "Truth". It is the depth of that bare honesty that makes up the true character of what we have become.

That depth in many a dish can only be found in stock. Stock is the character foundation to the evolution of what you finally present as an extension of yourself to your guests. I'm sure you have heard me say numerous times that "what you are serving is a direct representation of the person not only that you have become, but the person you hope to one day be". Do you really want your peers to view you as a man who takes short cuts in life? A proper stock gives body, flavor and an intriguing depth to the personality of the pot. It costs virtually nothing to make. Yet the treasures that will be yielded from your results of forethought and preparation will be priceless. Unfortunately, the end result of a great dish that displays the honesty of stock can not be acquired in a can or a carton or that cube of yellow salt. It is going to be something that you will have to make yourself with considerable gratification. As a side note, I have found those yellow cubes of bullion to be quite useful as a substitution for wagering dice.

The first lesson I will lend to your intellect is the importance of always purchasing meats that still have their bone attached. Even if you plan on cooking and serving your meats with out the bone, you can always carve it out yourself and save it to make stock another day. If you do plan on roasting your protein and serving it with the bone, don't assume a shy nature in not retrieving those bones after a meal. Those too, slowly coaxed in a pot will render wonderful results. I have often used the turkey carcass from one year to make the stock that provided the subsequent year's Thanksgiving gravy. It becomes a valuable lesson not just in cookery but in frugality and respect too. You are essentially transforming the kid that didn't get picked to play into the star of the team.

The soul of the bone lies in the gelatin. All bones, especially young bones and cartilage have a considerable amount of natural gelatin. It is this natural gelatin that lends all the tongue coating viscosity and body. For this reason, I tend to use a lot of feet in my stocks. The feet always have the highest ratio of cartilage to bone. Those little trotters are so incredibly inexpensive, I find it difficult not to procure a pack every time our paths intersect at the market. A package of feet in your store's cart along with a chin held high displays a formidable confidence to all mankind that may doubt your intentions in life.

The procedure for fashioning a stock that you can be proud of is very simple. The first thing you will need is a large sided pot. You must be able to fill the pot with a substantial amount of water allowing the bones plenty of space to submit their soul. If you are aiming for a dark stock, you must use bones that you have roasted until they are well caramelized in the oven. Likewise, the vegetables should take on the same caramelized traits as the bones. The vegetables that are the most polite to an accommodating stock are the yellow onion, celery and carrot. Place all of your bones and vegetables into the pot along with some accents of bay leaves, thyme and whole black peppercorns. A heavy dousing of red wine for you and the pot could only improve what will become a mundane situation. Fill the pot with water until it reaches 5 inches above your ingredients. Place your pot onto the stove and turn the flame on high. Go about your business and every 5 minutes or so, check on the progress of the pot. You will see some brackish grey foam rising from the depths of the vessel and finding a home on top of the liquid. These impurities must be removed with a spoon and discarded with conviction. They will cloud and taint your stock. A well constructed stock should be as clear and pure as a hug from your mother. When the pot begins to simmer, lower the heat. Allow the ingredients to gently dance along the bottom of the pot for 1 hour. Strain the stock and save in containers in your freezer or set it aside for some impeding use.

For a blonde stock, the only difference besides the obvious absence of roasting the bones, would be the cleaning of them. It is important to rinse the bones with a thought of removing any excess blood. The blood will keep your mother's hug from being so warm and comforting. A little white wine as opposed to red makes everyone happy and their teeth whiter too.

In regards to a stock of seafood, the elements of protocol remain the same. I do enjoy hacking the fish bones a little to expose the gelatin within the spine. Although I do suspect that it is unnecessary---it's just kind of cool to look at. I also prefer the roasting of the shellfish shells in the pot before including the rest of the orchestra. It seems to give the stock "Molto" personality. As if it didn't have enough to start.

The greater truth lies just beyond a pot, a few bones, some water and an hour of your care. Your life will never be as skewed from reality with the weight of a considerable stock always at your disposal.

Couchon Du Lait Po Boy
Serves 10

My close friend and accomplice in all illegal acts preformed in the search for our inner oenophile, Kuan Lim, was once given a whole hog as a gift. Lim is a gentleman of many talents and boundless intelligence. He can speak 5 languages, views billiards as "simple mathematics" and can successfully name not only the varietal of a new world white but tell you exactly where in California from hence it came. Cooking is an animal that presents quite a number of insurmountable problems. Once Lim poured all the dry contents of some instant Mac and Cheese into a pot and placed it over high heat. Neither the end result nor any other tales from Lim's cooking repertoire need to be mentioned. You know how that tale concludes.

It is in poor taste for anyone to refuse to partake in any foods cooked by their host. Fearful for my health and sense of well-being, I liberated not only that whole hog "gift" from Lim, but the immense weight of responsibility that was levied upon his unsuspecting soul. We all have our strengths and our unfortunate weaknesses. If Lim attends your party, for the love of God, put him in charge of the wine.

Couchon Du Lait Po Boy
1 Pork Butt with the bone
Blackening seasoning
1 yellow onion
3 stalks of celery
1 green bell pepper
8 cloves of garlic
2 cups white wine
3 bay leaves
2T thyme
1T oregano
1T basil
Creole mustard
thinly sliced red onion
4 loaves of French bread

Pre heat your oven to 325 degrees. Place your large Dutch oven, or if you hail from a more recent generation use your large Le Cruset, over high heat. Season the pork butt very aggressively with the blackening seasoning. Place the butt into the pot with the fat side down first. Continue to turn the pork around on all sides browning them evenly. Make sure the fat side is up and smother the pork with the onions, celery, bell pepper, garlic, wine and herbs. Bring to a simmer and cover the pork with a lid or some foil and place in the oven for 2 hours and 45 minutes. Uncover the pot and cook for an additional 30 minutes.

Take the pork out of the oven and let sit on the counter for about 30 minutes. While the pork starts to cool, cut the crusty ends off of the French bread. Retrieve a few of the braised garlic cloves and smear onto the bread. Look for where the rendered fat is floating in the pot and dunk your garlic bread into it. Share with no one!
Leaving the pork in the pot, use 2 forks and shred the meat. Taste the shredded pork and add salt or more blackening seasoning as needed. Cut the French bread lengths according to the size of your guest's individual appetite then cut the bread open as you would to resemble a clamshell. Spread a few layers of Creole Mustard onto the Po Boy bread. Load the inside of the Po Boy with the dripping shredded pork and a few of the red onion slices. I'm even brazen enough to spoon some extra of the pork nectar over the meat

before closing the Po Boy. Serve immediately at half time. You don't want the sins of a Po Boy getting in the way of sending up praise for the Saints.

****Many of the recipes in this book call for celery. Like all my ingredients, I never throw anything away. The leaves of the celery I save and use in a mix of lettuce. You can even use in place of an herb garnish for any meats of a light color.

Porcetta
Serves 8-10

I can easily see myself in Tuscany wobbling down the street with teeth stained red from wine and a face greased with the remnants of having attended a true Porcetta feast. Porcetta is a dish built from grand aspirations. You take a whole pig and completely remove the bones. Season the inside and roll it up to roast. The skin crisps as the belly fat renders onto the meat leaving multiple textures and flavors that arrive at each bite. My version spares the need for an expert butcher; all you need are a few expert eaters.

1 Center cut Pork Loin about 4-5 pounds
1 Skin on Pork Belly 4-5 pounds
12 cloves of garlic minced
1T ground fennel seeds
2 oranges zested
2T red pepper flakes
2T Kosher salt plus some extra to season properly
2t sugar
1T smoked paprika
1 bunch chopped Italian Parsley
1 1/2T chopped fresh rosemary

Start this adventure off by laying the pork belly down in front of you with the skin side up. Use a razor blade or a box cutter and score the skin in a criss-cross fashion. It takes a firm hand because the skin of a pig is thick from a childhood of verbal abuse. Flip the belly over so that the skin is down. In a small bowl, combine the garlic, fennel, orange zest, red pepper, salt, sugar, paprika, parsley and rosemary. Rub the spice mixture all over the belly and the loin. Lay the loin down the center of the belly and fold the sides of the belly around the loin. Flip the pig in a blanket over so that the seam is on the bottom. Pull out your butcher twine and start tying the package to ensure it holds while cooking. Tie each end first and then tie the middle. Fasten a few more stings in between the middle and the ends. Season the outside of the belly with some salt. If you need to ask how much then you probably shouldn't be attempting this feat. Place the tied pork on a pan and into your refrigerator uncovered for 2 days.

As each day goes by be sure to peek into your cooler and make sure your pork is still there. Like culinary alchemy, you have turned protein into gold and if your friends are even half interesting than they will be looking to steal it.

After the required 48 hours, take the pork out of the refrigerator and let it come to room temperature out on the counter for about 2 hours. Don't be hasty; you've already waited 2 days. Pre-heat your oven to 500 degrees. Place the Pork with the seam side down in a roasting pan and into the bottom 1/3 of your oven. Cook for 25 minutes and then lower the temperature to 325 degrees. Cook for an additional 2 ½ hours. Check the temperature by inserting a thermometer into the center of the loin. Once the gauge reads 140-145 degrees you are done. Remove the crackling pig from your oven and let it rest for about another 25 minutes. Feel free to snap little pieces of the crackling skin off and into your mouth while you wait.

Place the Porcetta onto a grand cutting board and slice using a serrated blade. The fat will be cascading down your knife and your hands will surely be coated in the porcetta's personality. Just lick your fingers in front of the audience and keep going. I'll be damned if any of your friends will turn any away.

****Some people get turned off by sharing off of common plates Not only they wont eat off a shared plate, but wont share their plate to you and yours. Those people should be ignored and abandoned. Or at least punched in the face.

David's Prawns
Serves 2

One of my absolute favorite things to eat is fried shrimp. This particular recipe is a take on a dish that I ate so frequently at a restaurant they named it after me. The brilliant part of this dish lay in the shrimp shells. The always discarded shells are left on the shrimp and turned so crispy during cooking its like eating a shrimp "chip".

1# of 10-15 size fresh Gulf Shrimp
1c cornstarch
Kosher salt
2c canola oil
1 leek white julienned
1 red bell pepper sliced thin
1 jalapeno sliced thin
4 cloves of garlic sliced thinly too

Time to dig through your pantry and retrieve the wok you bought and never had the nerve to use outside of your own imagination. But in your mind it really was quite the party and everyone sure was impressed.

51

Clean the shrimp by removing the heads first. Set them aside for later. Butterfly the crustacean by cutting down the back of the shrimp through the shell down to the tail and remove the vein. Season the shrimp along with the shrimp heads with some salt. Dust the shrimp and the heads with a solid coating of cornstarch.

Place the wok over high heat and add the oil. When the oil is hot, 360 degrees, add the shrimp heads. Fry the heads and toss them around giving them a good bath in the oil until they are golden and crispy. Remove the heads with a slotted spoon and add the shrimp to the wok. Now you really have the hang of it, take a picture and put it on one of those show off social sites for all to glare in awe. Once the shrimp are also cooked and crispy golden delicious, remove them and pour all of the super hot oil, EXCEPT 2 tablespoons, into a vessel that wont melt or a friend will post that pic and you'll be ruined. Return the wok that still has the 2T of oil in it back to the high heat flame and toss in the leek, bell pepper and jalapeno. Cook for 30 seconds. Add the garlic and return the shrimp and shrimp heads back to the wok. Toss over the high heat for 15 seconds and slide the whole mixture with the utmost grace onto a platter. Feast on the crispy shrimp vowing to never discard another shrimp shell again.

****I never remove the seeds from a jalapeno. That's like taking tackling out of football. Cooking chilies does tame the heat a bit. Sure, it still will be spicy but not in an intolerable way. Plus its proven to improve self-esteem issues.

Creole Jerk Grilled Ox Heart
Serves 6

I have always had trouble with shiny objects. They dart across my vision and the attention span follows right along with it. Cooking this dish can very well become a train wreck similar to a white boy trying to manage a professional wok. The marinade may take overnight but grilling meat on a stick is for your friends with the least ability to help you forge through this book. Save this recipe for them. Proper self-esteem is just fuel for a healthy appetite even though it may lend to overconfidence in the bedroom.

1lb grass fed ox heart
1/2c honey
1/2c soy
1T dried thyme
1bu scallion (chopped)
4 garlic cloves
1 habanero (stemmed)
1T ground allspice
1/2c orange juice concentrate
2T fresh ginger minced

Place the heart on your cutting board with no hesitation. Don't let the ox sense you are apprehensive or your palate will be gorged and punished by chewing what will seem to be forever. Trim the fat, veins and all of the sinew off of the meat. Pay attention to the ox and make paper-thin slices against the grain of the heart. Set the heart ribbons aside in a bowl or non-reactive container.

Take all of the rest of the ingredients and place in a blender. Puree the ingredients until nice and smooth. Pour the marinade over the heart and mix it around making sure all of your heart is thoroughly satiated. Repeat that step with some wine and your own heart. Cover the ox heart and set into the refrigerator overnight. Go ahead and also take about 25 wooden skewers and place them in a bowl or a plate covered with water.

As friends start to arrive the following day, light up the grill. Keep the lid closed on your grill allowing the grates to get very hot. Skewer the heart ribbons in a weaving fashion. Give the grates a little wipe with a cloth dampened with oil. Then lay the heart on a stick onto the grill. Char the heart on all sides and cook for 3-5 minutes. It would be best for your guests to be sitting outside with you. The aroma of charred beef and exotic spices will ignite a flood of salivitory gland activity. The world is a beautiful place when everyone is vying for your heart.

****This recipe is great with any cut of beef. Id go as far as to say the same for eggplant for the, GAST, vegetarians. I must be feeling really good today to say that. Does anyone need to borrow money?

Black Chicken Rillettes with Quail Egg Salad
Serves 1

Sense and Sensibility. Some days I am filled with one and some days I am filled with both. Some times I'm just filled with IT. But it is in the times of downtrodden depression that I seem to have the magical ability to conjure up neither. All of our recipes and journeys up to this point have been filled with luxury. But in a sly sort of way, our luxurious meals have still has been fairly economical. The Breast of Lamb recipe literally cost me $12 and it fed 4 people comfortably. The Rooter to The Tooter is luxury for the intelligent. Of coarse every so often we must throw caution to the wind and really splurge. What's the first thing one does when he has been asked not to return to his job? Buy $25 worth of Chinese black chicken to make rillettes that serves one, of coarse.

2 whole Chinese black chickens
2qts lard
Chinese five spice
1 can(15oz) of quail eggs
2T green onion chopped

T dill pickle relish
2T sweet pickle relish
2t fresh ginger minced
3T mayonnaise
Kosher salt
Bread
Olive oil

Take the whole birds and cut them into their respective pieces. Cut off the neck, then the legs and split the breasts. Place all the pieces into a pot and add the lard. Mark your flame to medium heat and after the lard has melted make sure all the pieces of chicken or fully submerged. What a wonderful fantasy those 2 chickens are living. As the fat starts to jiggle like my belly when I walk, turn down the heat to low. If the fat starts to jiggle like my belly when I dance, then the music is too loud and must be turned down. We are poaching not frying. Let the birds poach for 2 hours. Turn off the heat and let the black chickens cool in the fat.

Remove the birds from their fantasy of fat and pick all the meat and skin from the bones. The skin is fairly thin and so I see no reason not to invite it to the party too. Take 2/3rds of your chicken and shred it in a food processor until it is fine and smooth. Take the other 1/3 of your chicken and shred it by hand. Mix the 2 together and add some of the poaching lard until a smooth spreadable paste consistency is achieved. Add the salt just until it tastes slightly saltier than you want and the Chinese five spice to taste slightly more spiced than you want. The subsequent chilling will compensate your palate later on. Place the mixture into a crock and top with a layer of poaching fat. The fat will seal the rillettes from the oxygen and the bacteria that follows it. Chill the rillettes crock until the time comes.

Make the egg salad by rough chopping the quail eggs and mixing in a bowl with the green onion, relish, ginger and mayonnaise. A pinch of salt wouldn't hurt.
The chosen vessel for consumption is the crostini. I like the "chewiness" of frying as opposed to baking for this recipe. Cut some ½ inch thick slices of crusty artisan bread and get a ¼ cup of olive oil hot in a pan. Fry the bread on both sides until nice and brown and pile them up for later.

Gather your puppies and put them on your lap. Arrange the rillettes, bread and egg salad on the arm of your lazy boy. Give your gorgeous fiancé some pathetic look that will make her go fetch a bottle of wine. Can anything really be that bad?

"My "passion" for cooking is really just a symptom of my selfish compulsion for luxury".
                                        Me

The Necessity of Inspiration

A Line Cook's Flash back, 1992

"You aint fucking leaving until those racks are done". I gaze up to the wall as the sous chef punches out, grins and leaves. The 2 greased faces of the clock and mine meet, 12:37am. The holes that secure the buttons on my chef coat are no match for the pulling and tugging that it was tortured through a service of 300 diners. My chef coat unbuttons easy and then the stained apron goes back to protecting my T-Shirt and me. I need to keep my shirt somewhat clean for later. I don't want to look like a complete transient from the Westbank, who just so happened to stumble into an Uptown bar in hopes of mingling and scoring with some rich private college schoolgirl, because that would be the truth. Lying to girls is easy; lying to the plate is impossible.

I clock out and proceed to the walk-in. I get paid to cook but only from 2pm until 11pm. This is a 5 Bean restaurant and I know if I bust my ass hard enough this is the ticket out. My only certainty to a better life that extends beyond the Westbank lies along the unpaved road of sacrifice. If working off the clock is what I have to do to get ahead and get out, then like a man, I'm going to suck it up and do it. I pull the case of lamb racks off of the top shelf and carry the 40 pounds to my station. One by one I fly through racks by pulling off the fat cap and throwing it away before frenching the bones. That's good money going in the garbage, one day I'll do something magnificent with that fat cap. The sous chefs are always amazed at how fast I seem to get this task done. Of coarse I do, I'm not getting paid for it. The quicker I get out of here, the sooner I'm at a bar and the even sooner I am to meeting the drunk daughter of a wealthy Garden District resident. Either that or the Sous' girlfriend. The racks get placed into a large pan to marinate overnight and I tightly wrap the pan with clear plastic and place it back on the shelf of the cooler to await for my touch tomorrow.

The apron comes untied so easily, you would think it was trying to get rid of me and not the other way around. I let it fly through the air hitting the side of the dirty laundry bin before cascading to the floor. Screw it, no one is here and its late,,,,,,or is it early? Anyway, the dishwasher in the morning will come by and pick it up. I unfold my leather knife kit on top of the stainless steel table and place my boning and paring knives into their respective pockets. My steel goes in there too before enclosing the leather over the knives. I carefully place my 10-inch chef knife on top and wrap the other enclosed knives around it. This will leave the prized blade unsecured and the subsequent protruding handle will be ready for me to pull if there is any trouble on the path between the kitchen back door and my car that sits 4 blocks away. I place my wallet in my front pocket removing the last signs of opportunity for anyone that would think I was their lamb. Then I head to the back door.

The restaurant is in the CBD. Nestled snuggly in between an "INN" for denizens and a park for the homeless that don't have the 5 bucks to get in the Inn. Denizens are forever in great need of food, money and drugs. One look at this white boy and I may very well have all three. My step is filled with purpose paired with an expressionless face, as I look every person straight in the eye on the way to the car. I may be scared but I'm no coward. The evils looking to take anything that may be of value prey on cowards. Any man that won't look another man in the eye might as well paint a huge sign across his back "Gullible Provider!" I also keep a keen eye to the oncoming traffic. If I see a set of headlights stopped or moving slowly next to the cars parked along the sidewalk, I know trouble may have found me. Those headlights represent a true coward. A man with a Slim Jim that will quickly pop the lock of certain cars, preferably with no alarm, and within seconds any valuable contents inside your car will be inside his pocket as he pops the hood, jumps out and grabs your battery on the way back into his own vehicle. If I get to my car and the battery is gone, because only a complete idiot would leave personal belongings laying around, he better have driven off far and fast. My knife is ready and I'm not leaving here without my shit back. Hell, without a battery I can't!

Lamb Pancetta
Serves a lot

When you are passionate about something, your emotions will never let you forget. As an aspiring chef, my duty to the restaurant and an obligation to myself had me fabricating cases of racks of lamb each night. I'll never forget looking at the fat cap that covers the rack and how much it resembled unrolled pancetta. There are many thoughts that our mind will not let us erase. Here is one of the scant few good ones.

To attain a fat cap from the rack of a lamb, just ask your favorite aspiring chef. Most certainly they will either have one to give you or know someone who does. Increase your odds of getting the lamb in a timely manner by buying them a glass of wine.

The fat cap from 1 rack of lamb
2T pomegranate molasses
2T black peppercorns
1T coriander seeds
1T rosemary minced
1/4c Kosher salt
2t curing salt
3 garlic cloves minced

Take the fat cap and pat it dry. Rub the pomegranate molasses over both sides of the lamb. Grind the peppercorn and the coriander in your wife's trusty coffee grinder. Its okay for the grinder to not be completely clean. A little coffee will ensure this pancetta is original as well as the spices in her coffee the next morning. Mix the ground spices with the rosemary, salt and garlic. Spread the mixture over both sides of the lamb.
Place the lamb into a gallon size plastic bag and press out all the air before sealing. Lay the bag onto a sheet pan or in a baking dish with another pan on top. Use some of the

extra canned goods in your pantry to press down the lamb using the weight to help the spice's influence sway the meat into doing the right thing. Place the lamb into the refrigerator for 5 days worth of coercion.

Remove the lamb from the bag and give a quick rinse under some water. Pat it dry. If there are a few pieces of spice here or there still adhering to the meat, that is completely acceptable. Lay the lamb down in front of you with the meat side up and tightly roll up the mixture. Secure the roulade by tying butcher twine around the cylinder.
Find a place to hang the pancetta. You need a spot that hovers around 60 degrees and is free from sunlight. Perhaps hanging from a dreary basement or a bathroom shower curtain rod in bathroom that is never used. Maybe even your ex's heart would be fairly ideal.

Hang the pancetta for 2 weeks. It should emit a wonderful savory smell. If it starts to smell putrid, use some sense and throw it out. Take it down, and wrap in plastic wrap all the while storing in the refrigerator or freezer. Use whenever the occasion calls for you to show off being the only one to have rescued a piece of lamb from the garbage.

****This recipe is actually the manifestation of a dream. We may try and fail many times with our recipe aspirations. But as long as we never give up and keep dreaming, we will be forever happy.

Mint Spiced Lamb Breast with Skordalia
Serves 3

There are no binds that can confine an intuitive cook. Cooking can be just as full filling to the soul as Love when you learn to listen and hear your heart. Our hearts have been telling us what to eat and when to eat it since the day we were conceived. The Heart's woodwind section becomes overwhelmed with the incessant bombardment of the percussion that is the media. I am very apologetic because the heart cannot spin a soliloquy grand enough to be heard above the torture of the television's song.
Once we free ourselves from the couch and clear our minds with the smell of the seasons, we can really commit to the self-gratification that we deserve. I did not walk into the grocer with this recipe in mind. It presented itself and the intuition of my open heart told me to desire and acquire it. Cooking with the seasons is not a new concept that Jamie Oliver created. It is exactly the way things were before tomatoes had been modified to sell in December. I would even jest to propose the next time any of us go to a café that is selling an unadulterated raw tomato salad in December, we shall order it and throw it across the dining room. If there is a gentleman wearing linen there, then throw it at him and kill 2 birds with one stone. I got your Food Revolution right here Oliver.

3-3 1/2# of lamb breast
2T garlic cloves
1t ground coriander
1 1/2t ground cumin
1t cinnamon
1t ground ginger
1 1/2t red pepper flakes
1t Kosher salt
½ bunch of flat leaf parsley
1c mint leaves
1/2c extra virgin olive oil
2 lemons
2# baby potatoes
1c white wine
For the Skordalia
1 russet potato peeled and quartered
1/4c onion sliced
3 garlic cloves
1/3c extra virgin olive oil
¾-1c water

Take the garlic, coriander, cumin, cinnamon, ginger, red pepper, salt, parsley, mint, oil and the zest only of the 2 lemons and place it into a food processor. Process the mixture until a nice paste is created. Lay your lamb breast into a roasting pan and spread the mint spice paste evenly over the breast. Let the spice mixture massage the meat in your refrigerator overnight.

To make the Skordelia: Place the potato and onion into a properly salted pot of water and cook until the potato is tender. Drain the potato, reserving a cup of the liquid and place it into your cleaned food processor along with the garlic, the juice from one of the left over lemons, olive oil, and reserved potato broth. Process the Skordelia until it is smooth. Taste and add any salt needed. Go ahead and make a day ahead just to keep your hand free to make some cocktails during the final preparation of the lamb.

To cook the Lamb: remove it from the refrigerator and pre-heat your oven to 325 degrees. Using a dinner fork as your tool, impale the baby potatoes a few times. Make a sufficient mattress of potatoes and lay the lamb breast on them in a roasting pan. Pour the cup of wine into the pan and cover the pan with some foil. Place the roasting pan into your oven and cook for 2 ½ hours. Make a few cocktails too keep the heat of the pending summer at bay. Remove the foil from the pan and cook for an additional 30 minutes with a raised heat of 375 degrees. Take the pan out of the oven and let the meat rest for as long as your constitution will allow. Cut a few of the lamb ribs from the breast and serve with a fine dollop of the Skordelia and a few of the potatoes bathed in the drippings of the lamb. Be sure not to wash your hands that night. One of mornings great pleasures is the aroma of lamb fat and mint still lingering from your fingers.

****I have a huge problem with the term "Farm to Table" or "California Cuisine" as a modern concept. That is implying that before food media, Alice Waters and Brooklyn tattoos every chef's goal was to find the least freshest food available and serve it. That's just insulting.

Pain Perdu Farci: Bacon Jam Stuffed French Toast
Serves 4

The most important meal of the day is breakfast. It is utterly impossible to become a productive man making sound intelligent decisions without starting off the day with sugar, caffeine and liquor. The thrust of these three social lubricants will not only make the sky open up from the sense of your well being, but you will find the annoyances of mankind more tolerable. Be mindful in not taking in so much lubricant to where you start to exchange "tolerable" with "excusable". Bourbon may first give a sharpening of your tongue. But without any moderation it will then take any compassion you have for the souls less fortunate than yourself----and there are many. I am steadfast assure of this fact because you are reading my ramblings instead of watching Guy Fieri stick his gaudy jewelry all over some food he is preparing to seduce some poor soul's wallet. Anyone looking to buy a Lamborghini?

For the Bacon (Who's your Umami) Jam
3lbs bacon cut into random pieces
½ large yellow onion rough chopped
6 cloves garlic
1 1/2c white wine preferably a gewürztraminer
1/4c soy sauce
1/2c Louisiana cane syrup
3 bay leaves
2T shiitake powder (can be made with a coffee grinder and a few dried mushrooms from your local Asian market)
2c water
3/4c dark brown sugar
For the Syrup
1 1/2c Louisiana cane syrup
1c chicory coffee
To Assemble
3 eggs
1/4c milk
1 shot or so, or so, of fine bourbon
8 slices of French bread
1 stick of unsalted butter
Spiced pecans (recipe can be found in the chicken gizzard confit posting)

59

For the bacon jam: This will make 6 nice pint jars of jam to give to a loved one or to bribe a publisher to print your cookbook. Either way it is a score. Place a large pot onto the stove and put in all of the listed ingredients. Cover the pot and bring it to a confident simmer. Cook the jam for 20 minutes in the covered pot. Remove the lid, slightly turn up the heat and cook an additional 25 minutes or until the mixture has been reduced by half. When the jam starts to love on the bottom of the pot a bit too much, scrape it with a wooden spoon and be assured that you are done. Take off the heat and let cool a bit. Remove the bay leaves and process the jam in an electric food processor. Evenly divide the jam into your sealable jars and set in the cooler until needed.

For the syrup: bring the sole 2 ingredients to a simmer and reduce by half in a small pot for 10-12 minutes. Let cool and it will thicken on its own account.

To finish the dish, whisk the eggs with the milk and bourbon. Generously spread some jam onto one piece of bread. Place another piece of bread on top entrapping the jam. I shouldn't have to say it, but I will, repeat for the rest of the bread slices. Place the stuffed pain perdu into the egg mixture allowing it to soak in the pleasure of a freshly laid egg, not dissimilar to the way your loved one acts in a shower of your complements. Put a cast iron or non-stick skillet over medium heat and place a common sense worth's pat of butter into the skillet. Cook the Pain Perdue until it is wonderfully brown on both sides and warmed all the way through. If you tend to cut the bread very thick you might want to continue the heating in the oven. Place the Pain Perdue onto a plate and shower it with complements of syrup and spiced pecans. Don't make the mistake of dusting with powdered sugar. That's just uncalled for and too messy for the mid-morning.

"In good times people want to drink, In bad times they have to."
Me

The Treatment and Mistreatment of Fish

First if you can offer some savory bait
The likes of which it has never before tasted and never will again—
A scrap of cow's liver, or some airborne, iridescent insect—
in which to hide the gleaming hook

Catch at least two so none must await death alone in the bucket
Change the water
Dispatch them quickly with a sharp knife rocked firmly over the smiles of gills
Remember, Dr. Guillotin believed his invention one of mercy
Do not flinch, reserve the heads for stock

Scrape off the flakes of silver armor with the backside of your knife,
so as not to damage the skin.
Hold your thumb against the zipper teeth of the spine
as your forefinger directs attention from the body.
Slice open the belly.
Give the guts to the cat surely slinking around your ankles.

Offer no insult of breadcrumb or eggwash.
Rinse until all runs clear of blood
Pat dry, gently, as you would a lover's tears or a child's bottom.
Sprinkle with fragrant herbs, a soupcon of fluer de sel,
One wrist-twist of white pepper, no more.
Lay it to bed in a pan of warm butter,
And mourn until the flesh falls off the bone.

M. N. Altenderfer

Whole Roasted Salmon cooked in the *Times Picayune Newspaper*
Serves 8

Every now and then it is necessary to show out. Demand the spotlight on stage, preach from the altar and impale the mountain with your flag. I was going to say this is one of those recipes that allows and even demands such action. But in retrospect, all of the recipes in this book do just that. The next time you are sarcastically asked "How does it feel to be better than everyone else?" You earnestly respond "GREAT".

1 Whole 4lb salmon cleaned and gutted
2 oranges sliced paper thin
Sorrel pesto (see recipe)

1 lobe of foie gras cut into 2 inch slices (optional)
olive oil
Kosher salt
4 black and white ONLY sheets of newspaper. Colored ink can some times be toxic and toxic personalities are only invited to parties serving white zinfandel over ice no less.

Sorrel Pesto
4c sorrel chopped
4 garlic cloves
1/2c slivered almonds (toasted)
t salt
1/2c shredded parmesan
1/2c olive oil

It is time to secure your right as the Master of your Domain. Take the salmon along with your best flexible filet knife and lay them in front of you. Our intention is to debone the fish while leaving it whole and intact. I do not possess the genetic defect that causes one to be left-handed; I am a right-handed individual. So these instructions are for the masses. Just flip the script if you are a lefty.

Lay the salmon on a cutting board with the belly facing you and the head to the right. Insert your knife with the blade pointing to the tail just inside of the opened gut and on top of the spine. Don't be nervous or afraid. Any signs of an unsteady blade will never show since the gauged meat will always stay on the inside of the fish. Guide your blade down the spine until you reach the tail. The belly will be cut open but do not pierce the skin that crests the back. Think of a book with the crest of the back representing the binder. Take your blade, starting in the same place; just send the knife towards the tail under the spine this time. At the end of the tail, turn your blade and cut through the spine. Now we are going to free the fish from the front half of the skeleton. Turn and flip the fish so that the head is to the left and the open book of the belly is facing you. Insert your knife into the same spot as when you started---in the belly and above the spine. During this step, when you guide the knife down the spine towards the head you will be confronted with the rib cage of the fish. Just simply use the top of your filet knife and use the rib cage as a guide to separate the meat from the bone by cutting along the bone towards yourself. Do that motion in waves until you reach the head. Use the same principle of not cutting through the crest of the back. Repeat the step in separating the spine and rib cage from the fish's meat for the bottom of the fish that leads up to the head. When you reach the head this time, turn your blade vertical and cut through the spine. At this point the spine should be completely freed from the salmon's flesh and you can slide it right on out. Save that bone for stock on another day.

The final step in your mastery of the poissonier position is to simply remove the pin bones. Fetch the tweezers used to keep your face nicely framed by your eyebrows. Run your fingers down the inside of the flesh starting near the head and go down to the tail. Each time you feel a bone, pluck it out as any great metrosexual would do.

Make the pesto by placing all the ingredients into a food processor and just turn it on. Puree the pesto until it is smooth. Superior flavor can be had with a mortar and pestle. But after dominating the fabrication of the salmon, you really don't have anything to prove. Especially considering by now your friends have probably poured you your third glass of Alsace.

Pre-heat the oven to 425 degrees. Sprinkle the inside of the cavity with a knowledgeable hand of salt. Take the pesto and fill the cavity with a nice smooth layer. Then use one of the oranges and layer the bottom of the inside of the salmon. Allow the oranges to overlap ensuring none of the bottom side is unadorned with citrus. If you have optioned to be absurd, lay the foie gras in the center of the salmon from head to tail. Get your assistant or someone you have a crush on to do the last layer of oranges over the top of the foie gras mimicking the fine work you did on the bottom.

Once again, take your knowledgeable hand and season the complete outside of the salmon with salt. Moisten your 4 pieces of newspaper with some water and lie out in front of you. Place the salmon in the middle. Fold all 4 ends of the newspaper up, completely enclosing the fish. Turn the parcel so the seam side is down and place on a baking tray. Slide the fish en papillote into the oven and roast for 50 minutes. Use some sense, if your fish is a bit heavier like your aunt, then cook a little longer. If it is a little lighter, then cook a little less.

Remove the fish from the oven and place in the center of a table built for grandeur. Tear open the newspaper and slice as needed. Keep the collar and the cheeks for yourself for your guests need none of the lagniappe. If they aren't satisfied with your presence and that of the salmon, F them!

****When making any kind of pesto, it is best to add all the ingredients except the green herb into the food processor first and give it a run. Then add the green herb last. The oil that is already in the processor will keep a lot of the oxygen off of the herb during the cutting, hence helping it not oxidize—turn brown.

Chapter 5 Foot and Fin

The Significance of Traveling

One of the most significant things we do in life is travel. Absorbing the smells, sights, sounds, noises and tastes of a foreign land during a sojourn can only be rivaled by making love. It all translates into a hand that completely guides the subconscious into peeling the onion that is our palate, revealing more layers than we thought we possessed. Show me a man that does not leave his immediate vicinity and I'll bet his cooking is garnished with chopped curly parsley, he drinks Beaujolais nouveau in June and has quite the collection of tube socks. A joke has a head and a butt, which are you?

For every positive, there is obviously a negative, for every action, an equal and opposite reaction. The Yin and Yang if you will. That's what life is about, balance. I have been fortunate to travel extensively in my post adolescence. That ability to travel was exactly how professional cooking got me drunk, lured me into her arms and took advantage of me---and still does. I must admit when it comes to traveling, I am a complete prostitute. I'm talking the nasty, addicted and living under a bridge type, not the cute Julia Roberts/Richard Gere Pretty Woman kind. This addiction has led me to be the better man and cook by ten fold because of it!

But there is a dark side to it all. What connection do I have to any particular physical place? I am very connected to my wife, child and dogs Rooter and Tooter. I love and feel connected to cuisine and all that it represents as well the ideals held forth by The Southern Foodways Alliance. If I am indeed anything it is Creole. My food, demeanor, hospitality and liver all denote Creole. Just like Creole, my personality is a gumbo of many different values all put together out of a necessity to survive in the most practical and yet pleasurable way possible. It's that whole Yin and Yang thing again.

Would I feel a sense of place or home in Barcelona, Provence or Bali? Probably. But New Orleans is a well-traveled Madame herself. I, like her, have become the sum of all my experiences. When you sit at either of our tables, your palate and your heart will savor all of our exploits. Traveling has built a piano for us to play that just happens to have a few more keys. You don't really want to be considered a man that cooks with flat musical tendencies. After all, isn't the goal to be like Richard, Julia on the piano?

Fried Fish Fins with Carolina Vinegar Sauce
Serves as many people as you have fins to cook

The first time a Creole chef gave me a fried fish fin to eat I thought it was a joke. I am a butt of many things; his jokes weren't to be one of them. But James Inwood wasn't one of those kinds of gentlemen. He was thoughtful and very open with his knowledge to a pestering young cook. Life has numerous steps that lead you to today. His directional push 25 years ago could be the single reason this book is here today.

Fresh Fish Fins, flounder is best
cornstarch
Kosher Salt
black pepper
Carolina Vinegar Sauce (see recipe)

As you can see from the lack of measurements, I'm embarrassed to even write this recipe. There are so many recipes in this book that require not only a decent understanding of the table but of yourself too. So come on, season, dust and fry until crispy. Douse with vinegar and enjoy. If that's too hard then look me up, come by and I'll hold your hand while you go to the bathroom.

Carolina Vinegar Sauce
1 bottle of your favorite wine
1 1/2c cider vinegar
1/2c ketchup
1/2c water
1T sugar
1t kosher salt
1t red pepper flakes

Drink the bottle of wine. Save the bottle and rinse it out. Mix all the goodies together and pour it into the wine bottle. Store in a cool place. A few days is great. Use any time you want spice and some acidity.

"Hard work is for people with no talent"
George Carlin

Pig Foot Jelly

Do not underestimate the power of this jelly. It will take any dish that is lacking soul and give it purpose. An untrained palate would think this to be a waste if they were to taste it naked--as in unadulterated. But to the savvy lover, this jelly will open the door to potential you didn't think existed in your food and even in yourself. Making this with a crazy sexy young girl that was and still is out of my league is what made her my wife. "You had me at pig foot".

10 pig feet
2 yellow onions
1 head of garlic split in half
2T black peppercorns
3 bay leaves
3 stalks of celery

1 bottle of Madeira
T kosher salt
A dozen preserving jars

Place all of the ingredients into a very large pot and cover with cold water. Only the chill of the water will coax the soul (gelatin) out of the bones. Hot water will just scare it and trap it in forever. Turn the heat to its most intense flame and watch for the pot to come to a simmer. Collect any scum that will accumulate at the top of the broth and discard it or save it for the dogs. I will put it on top of Rooter and Tooter's, my 2 dogs, food all the time. Pig feet have a way with casting enchantment.

Once the pot is simmering, lower the heat and just forget about it for 2-3 few hours. Turn the heat off and let cool for 20-30 minutes. Just because I was always in a rush to burn myself during my professional career doesn't mean you should be. Remove the feet from the broth to a pan. Let cool a bit more. Once the feet are cool enough to handle, pick through them removing all the bones and reserving all the meat and skin. Your hands will become glazed with the joys of sticky gelatin. This is the same joy that coats the tongues of your guests and separates you from mediocrity. I have little concern over where your mouth has been; feel free to lick your hands as you go. Chop the meat and skin and place some in each of your sanitized jars, not that I have any concern over where your jars have been. Then strain the hot liquid through a fine mesh strainer and pour into the jars. Seal the jars then place the sealed jars into the cooler.

The next day, make sure all the "buttons" have caved inward. If any have not, then just get it all hot and give another shot at resealing. Anytime I feel the need to add a boost of personality to any sauce, I pull out a jar and liberally spoon some into the pan while I reminisce over the most beautiful woman in the world flirting with me and my pig foot jelly.

****If I have said it once, I have said it a million times, women love a guy that can cook. It is the great physical equalizer. Now if you possess humor on top of that, the world is your oyster.

Canard et Conserve: Duck in a Can
Serves 4

This is my interpretation of the great Chef Martin Picard's dish of Duck in a Can. I had won an award for being a *Chef To Watch* by Louisiana Cookin Magazine along with a few other chefs for 2008. My prize was to cook the main dish at an event for charity with the other winners. Chef Picard is a consummate lubricated showman and my man crush would push me in the same direction. If you are going to be on stage then you might as well give them a show.

This dish has confit, cabbage, pepper jelly and foie gras. Any time you dump that out of a can, applause and endless adoration will soon follow.

For the Duck Confit:
4 duck legs
10 sprigs fresh thyme
4 cloves of garlic
4 bay leaves
1/2c Kosher salt
1/4c sugar
T ground coriander
t cinnamon
Duck fat to cover the legs
For the Smothered Cabbage:
4 strips bacon dices
1 yellow onion sliced
2 cloves of garlic minced
2T fresh thyme leaves
1t ground juniper berries
1 head of cabbage shredded
1/2c chicken stock
For the Pepper jelly:
1 orange zested and juiced
2 ancho chiles toasted, seeded and ground
2c rice vinegar
1qt light corn syrup
1/2oz powdered gelatin
1 red bell pepper minced
To Assemble:
4 10oz Aluminum cans and lids or substitute jars
4oz Foie Gras sliced
Cracklins for garnish

To Make the Confit: Press the thyme, bay leaves, and garlic on the meat side of the duck leg. In a stainless steel bowl, mix together the salt, sugar, coriander, and cinnamon. Turn the leg over and liberally coat the skin of the legs with the salt mixture. Place the legs on a pan and cover the pan with some plastic wrap. Place the pan into the refrigerator for 2 days. Remove the legs from the pan and rinse the salt and herbs off the legs. Pat the legs dry and place in a pot, skin side down. Cover the legs with the duck fat and cook on lowest possible fire, allowing the legs to slowly bubble for 90 minutes. Cool legs in fat until ready to use.

To make the Cabbage: In a medium-size pot render the bacon on low heat until lightly browned. Add the onion and cook for 8 to 10 minutes. Add the garlic and cook for 1 minute. Add the thyme, juniper, cabbage, and chicken stock to the pot. Cover the pot and cook for 30 minutes or until the cabbage is tender. Season with salt and pepper to taste.

For the Pepper Jelly: In a medium pot, place the orange juice and zest, ground ancho, vinegar, and corn syrup on a medium flame and bring to a simmer. Bloom the gelatin by placing it in 2 tablespoons cold water, and add it to the pot. Stir until the gelatin is dissolved. Turn off the heat and add the red bell pepper. Place in a container and let cool.

To Assemble: Season foie gras with salt and pepper. Sear the foie gras in a very hot skillet until nicely browned on both sides. Set aside to cool. Pour 2 ounces of pepper jelly into the bottom of a 10-ounce can or mason jar. Place a boned duck leg into the can and insert the foie gras into the middle of the duck leg. Top the can off with the cabbage and seal the can or jar. Repeat steps until all cans or jars are filled. At this point the cans or jars can be held under refrigeration until needed.

To serve, place the sealed cans in a pot of boiling water for 20 minutes. If you are using jars they will need to be warmed up before putting in the boiling water. Allow the jars to warm to room temperature for about 20 minutes and then place them under warm to hot running water until they are warm to the touch before placing in the boiling water. Take the can out of the boiling water and let sit for 5 minutes. Open the can and with a flourish of dramatics, place the contents of the can in a bowl and stud the plate with cracklins for texture. Raise a glass to your health, hard work, and to me—cause boy do I need it.

"You can trust a skinny chef. Never trust a chef with an ugly mate"

Me

Roasted Pig Foot stuffed with Crawfish Jambalaya

Serves 4

After a certain amount of dues are paid, there is little that impresses one's self anymore. It becomes like a bad marriage when everything gets taken for granted. I have done it for so long I expect the cuisine I create to be great every single time. Incredible meals are the boring norm and talent is lowered to just another side note in life until I made this. The flavor really had less to do with what I put in it and more to do with the contribution of the trotter. A good swift kick in the gastronomic butt by a pig was all I needed for proper perspective.

4 whole pig feet
1 yellow onion chopped large
2 celery stalks
1 garlic head cut in half
6 sprigs of thyme
2c white wine
1T black peppercorns
2 bay leaves
1T kosher salt
For the Jambalaya stuffing:
2T olive oil

1c yellow onion minced
1/2c celery minced
1/2c green bell pepper minced
2T garlic minced
1T dried thyme
2t dried oregano
2t dried basil
1 bay leaf
2t cayenne pepper
2c Louisiana popcorn rice
4c reserved pig foot cooking broth
1bu green onion sliced thin
8oz fresh Louisiana crawfish tails (frozen is OK but imported is not)
Caul fat

The first step is to poach the pig feet. Take the feet and score the foot with a sharp knife. Cut one straight line from the "palm" down the foot to the ankle. When the foot revolts from the heat, it will naturally tear in random spots. Scoring the foot will force the tear to happen where we tell it. Place the feet, onion, celery, garlic, thyme wine, black peppercorns, bay leaves and salt into a pot that is obviously big enough to hold all of the ingredients. Turn on a flame to its highest setting and put the pot over it bringing it to a low simmer. Skim the scum as it rises to the top of the pot and simmer the feet for an hour and 20 minutes. Turn the flame or glowing electric spiral burner off.

Take the feet out of the pot and let them chill just long enough to be able to handle without being in pain, unless you're into that sort of thing. Pick all the bones out of the feet having a careful hand that makes sure the skin doesn't get torn up too much more. Every now and then a bone you pick out will have some meat or cartilage attached. Pick any meat and cartilage still attached to the bone off and set it aside for the jambalaya. Go ahead and set aside the cleaned feet too and have a glass of wine. Just typing this is making my palate parched.

Strain the pot in which the feet were cooked and save the nectar.

For the Jambalaya: Pull a medium sized pot out of your cabinet. Grab one that you know were the lid is located. If anyone is watching, spin the pot around like one of those studs on *Iron Chef* and place it on the stove. Turn that knob to high heat and add the olive oil. When the oil waves some smoke at you, that's the signal to add the onion. Sprinkle the onion with a pinch of salt in order to season as we go, providing proof that we are indeed intelligent. Cook the onion for 2-3 minutes then add the celery. Stir the pot and cook the celery for another minute. Swipe the bell pepper and garlic off of your cutting board and into the pot along with the dried herbs and cayenne pepper. Cook and stir some more for another minute. Add the rice and any of the picked pig feet meat and cartilage to your pot and stir that around making sure this party is properly mingled. Pour in the 4 cups of reserved pig foot broth and bring to a simmer. Taste the broth as it comes to a simmer and add more salt as needed. The rice will absorb the flavors with quite a bit of greed, so be certain to make your broth taste slightly salty. Once the pot is simmering, turn the burner down to a very low flame and cover the pot. Cook for 20 minutes. Turn the pot off and take the lid off. Dump the jambalaya out of the pot and into a large bowl. Fold the crawfish tails and green onion into the jambalaya and let the stuffing cool in the refrigerator.

To stuff the feet, lay each trotter down in front of you and amply fill the inside with some jambalaya. It will fall out a little here and there and that's ok. The Caul fat will hide all the imperfections. Lay the caul fat out flat and cut a square piece that your good sense says is plenty big enough to wrap one of the feet. Place a stuffed foot on the front portion of the caul fat closest to you running in a left to right direction. Leave 4 or 5 inches of fat in between you and the foot. Take the edge of the caul fat closest to you and fold it over the foot. Then fold the sides of the fat over the 2 edges of the foot and tightly roll it away from you. It's the same technique as rolling a burrito, eggroll or Vietnamese spring roll. If you haven't done any of those things then you need to get out more. Repeat with all of the feet.

To Serve: Preheat the oven to 425 degrees. Place a large non-stick or cast iron skillet on the high heat. Season the stuffed feet with salt and pepper. Glaze the pan with a touch of fat (Artists choice). When the pan smokes add the feet into it. Brown the feet on all sides. Make sure the seam of the caul fat is facing down into the pan for each foot and place the pan into the oven. Cook in the oven for 8-10 minutes. Remove from the oven and place the pan on a trivet in front of your guests. Watch how many of them burn their mouths because they simply can't wait for it to cool to get another bite. Yes, it is that good.

****You can serve the jambalaya just as it is if you wish. We fold the crawfish in at the end to be sure they don't get chewy from being overcooked. But you could choose to use shrimp and add the raw ones with the stock. All Creole and Cajun rice dishes have green onion added to the end. The textural bite of the raw onion is a extremely significant detail.

Pot Au Feu

Pot Au Feu is the quintessential French family meal. It celebrates the rich and the poor, the summer and the winter and even the land and the air. I would venture as far as to say "Sea" too, but I wouldn't be fooling anyone---that's Bouillabaisse.
The foundation of the Pot au Feu, the stock, is by far the most important determining factor to which kind of Pot Au Feu you should create. Look into your freezer and see which stock it has you have the most of, from there, go about buying the various cuts of inexpensive meats needed. The same can be said for the accompanying vegetables. Your obviously not going to look in your freezer but on the shelves of the market.

The Technique

The players singing may change but the chorus remains the same. Start off by placing all of your meats into a large pot. Cover the meats with cold water and bring to a boil over high heat. The second the water starts to bubble turn off the heat and retrieve the meats. DUMP out the water and clean the pot. Yes, this may sound a bit anal-retentive but we tend to joyously be that way when true friends will be present. Place the meats back into the pot along with the herbs and seasoning vegetables. Pour your appropriate reserved stock into the pot and place over a high Feu. When the pot comes to a simmer, lower the heat and season with some Kosher salt to taste. Continue to cook very gently for 2 ½ hours. Constantly skim the surface of your Pot au Feu removing any foam and scum that may float to the surface. Just because purity isn't inherently in our heart doesn't mean it shouldn't be the dominant character we give to the pot. Add your finishing vegetables and cook an additional 30 minutes. Turn the heat off, arrange the meats and vegetables on a platter and ladle some of the broth around the platter. Serve with mustard and crusty bread on the side. Then be as brash as to ladle the broth into teacups allowing your friends to toast and drink to their pure hearts.

Classically, no stock is used to fortify the Pot Au Feu. So if you live your life as a C-student and have no stock on hand, just use water. When your friends call you out on it, cite nostalgia and tradition as your motive.

Beef Pot Au Feu
6 pieces of ox tail
1lb of brisket
6 short ribs with bone in (salted lightly overnight)
6 marrow bones
Seasoning Vegetables
1 yellow onion peeled and studded with 6 cloves
1 bunch leeks whites only
3 carrots peeled and cut with your better judgment
1 small celery root peeled and cut into wedges
1lb brown mushrooms
1 Bouquet Garni of Thyme, tarragon and bay leaves
1 Sachet containing 1T each of whole black and white peppercorns
Finishing vegetables:
10 small Yukon gold potatoes
1 head of cabbage cored and cut into wedges

Garnish
1lb flank steak cut very thinly against the grain***
Creamy Horseradish Mustard (see recipe)
Thick slices of crusty bread

***Lay the raw flank steak along the bottom of the serving platter along with the meats and vegetables. Pour the hot broth over the raw meat just before serving.

Creamy Horseradish Mustard
1c mayonnaise
3T Dijon mustard
1/4c sour cream
1T horseradish
Mix together the ingredients and place in a bowl to serve with the Pot Au Feu.

Pork Pot Au Feu
2 Ham Hocks
1lb pork belly
1lb pork butt (salted overnight)
2 pig feet

Seasoning Vegetables(Only simmer this step for 1 hour and 30 minutes)
1 yellow onion peeled and halved
1 bunch leeks whites only cut in half lengthwise
3 carrots peeled and cut with your better judgment
1 small celery root peeled and cut into wedges
1 bunch collard greens washed, stemmed and cut into thick strips
Bouquet Garni of Bay leaves, thyme and a chunk of ginger
Sachet containing 1T each of whole black and white peppercorns, whole coriander, red pepper flakes and 2 star anise

Finishing Vegetables
1lb fresh lima beans
4 ears of corn cut into 1/3rds
4 links of Boudin blanc or boudin noir (do both for a boost to your manhood)

*Garnish****
Cabbage sliced thin
Sweet potato mustard (see recipe)
Thick slices of crusty bread

**** Use the raw cabbage by serving it with the broth as an opening soup course.

Sweet Potato Mustard
1 large sweet potato
1/2c creole mustard
2T honey

Poke a few holes into the sweet potato and lightly coat it with canola oil. Bake the potato in the oven at 425 degrees for 45 minutes or until soft to the touch. Let the potato cool and scoop out the flesh. Mix with the mustard and honey and a pinch of salt. Mother Nature doesn't grow uniform sweet potatoes. You may need a bit more mustard. Taste it. Does it taste like an equal marriage of sweet potato and mustard?

Veal Pot Au Feu

4 veal shanks

1 veal cheek

1lb veal neck with bones cut into manageable pieces

Seasoning Vegetables

1 yellow onion peeled and halved

1 bunch leeks whites only cut in half lengthwise

3 carrots peeled and cut with your better judgment

1 small celery root peeled and cut into wedges

1 head of garlic cut in half

1 bulb of fennel cut into quarters

1lb white mushrooms

Bouquet Garni of Bay leaves, thyme and sage

Sachet containing 1T each of whole black and white peppercorns, fennel seeds and juniper berries

2c Riesling wine

Finishing Vegetables

1 rutabaga peeled and diced into peasant style chunks

2 turnips peeled and diced

1lb green peas

Garnish***

Mustard Vert (see recipe)

Thick slices of crusty sourdough bread

Whole radishes

Softened salted butter

***Interchange the butter, mustard, bread and radishes in an orgy like abandon.

Mustard Vert

1/2c mint

1/2c tarragon

1c flat leaf parsley

1T capers

1/2c Dijon mustard

2 anchovies

2 garlic cloves

1c olive oil

Place all except the oil into your food processor. Puree the ingredients and add the oil to combine into a smooth puree.

Don't ignore the lagniappe parts that come inside our ducks. Be sure to reserve everything when you clean the ducks. It all gets added sooner or later. Every kid deserves the chance to play.

Duck Pot Au Feu

4 duck drumsticks (skin removed and set aside for cracklin garnish)
4 duck thighs (skin removed and set aside for cracklin garnish)
2 duck backs
4 duck wings
Seasoning Vegetables (only simmer this step for 1 hour)
1 yellow onion peeled and halved
1 bunch leeks whites only cut in half lengthwise
3 carrots peeled and cut with your better judgment
1 small celery root peeled and cut into wedges
1 head of garlic cut in half
Bouquet Garni of Bay leaves, thyme and oregano
Sachet containing 1T each of whole black and white peppercorns, dried basil and red pepper flakes
Finishing Vegetables (bring to a simmer for only 10 minutes)
1lb cooked white beans
1 head napa cabbage cored and cut into large pieces
4 parsnips peeled and cut into chunks
1lb Andouille
4 duck breasts
Confit duck gizzards (see recipe)
Duck hearts

Garnish
8oz Foie Gras cut into 1 inch cubes***
Duck cracklins (see recipe)
Mustard Piquant (see recipe)
Thick slices of crusty bread
***Use the Foie gras by adding it to the broth and serve as the opening soup coarse.

Duck Cracklins
Slice the skin of the duck into thin strips and place in a non stick skillet that you can go ahead and put into a 350 degree oven. Stir the duck skin every so often until lightly brown. Remove from the oven and take out of the pan to cool. Season with a sprinkling of salt.

Mustard Piquant
6 cloves of garlic
Livers from the 2 ducks (cook in a skillet over high heat until done)
1/4c Dijon mustard
2t quatre epices
1T red wine vinegar
1/2c olive oil (or 1/2c fat left over from making the cracklins)
Kosher salt to taste
Puree the garlic, livers, mustard, quatre epices in a food processor until smooth. Add the vinegar then the oil to the running machine until done. Season with salt and pepper to your exquisite taste.

Duck Gizzard Confit
1 pint of duck gizzards
1T kosher salt
1T sugar
2 torn bay leaves
6 sprigs of thyme
1 pint of rendered duck fat

Season the gizzards with the salt, sugar, bay leaves and thyme. Place in a container to cure overnight. Rinse the gizzards and pat dry. Put them into a small pot and cover the gizzards with the duck fat. Place over a small flame and poach the gizzards very slowly for 2 hours. You want the fat to barley bubble as it dances with the gizzards. Any more than that and the slam dance will ensure a tough gizzard with too many firm political opinions. Let cool and store in the fat until needed.

Bone Marrow with Escargot, Green Peppercorn Bordelaise and Rosemary Beignet
Serves 4

In my shaving kit I always carry an oyster knife, cheese knife and 8 marrow spoons. I do feel I lead a pretty good life and the fact I consider marrow spoons a necessity bearing the same weight as a toothbrush is certain proof. I have to keep reminding myself how good I have it. I always thought the only true measure to a great life was tan feet. Mine are as white as a fish belly.

For the Beignets:
¾ cup water
1 Tablespoon yeast
1 egg
1 5oz can evaporated milk
3 ½ cups flour
1 Tablespoon shortening
1 Tablespoon sugar
pinch of salt
1 Tablespoon fresh rosemary chopped

For the Bordelaise Sauce:
2 Tablespoons of olive oil
2 shallots minced
3 cloves of garlic minced
1 cup of mushrooms minced
1 cup burgundy wine
2 Tablespoons of green peppercorns
1 bay leaf

1 cup veal demi glace

Butter
2 dozen snails
4 marrow bones

To make those wonderful pillows of fried dough, mix the luke warm water with the yeast and let the yeast wake up for 5 minutes in the warm throws of the waters hugs. In a separate bowl introduce the egg and evaporated milk to each other with a firm whisking. In yet a third bowl, mix together the rest of the dry ingredients. Add the milk to the yeast by mixing. Then add the whole liquid mixture into a nice well formed in the flour. Stir the liquid around the well collapsing the walls of flour until the dough starts to form. Add a touch more flour if needed to keep the dough cohesive onto itself and not the sides of everything it touches. Knead the dough with the palms of your hands on a table never opening your fist. The dough at this point is a young and impetuous thief and will snatch any ring right off your finger the moment you let it seduce you into opening your hand. Show some resolve and discipline by keeping your hand closed and kneading until you can poke it and the dough springs immediately back at you. Cover the dough letting it rest, mature and double in size while you turn your attention to the saucepot.

For the Sauce: place the olive oil into a small pot over a medium flame. Sweat the shallots for a few minutes while seasoning them with a pinch of salt the way any decent cook would. Add the garlic to the pot and cook for another minute. Place the mushrooms in the pot and cook while stirring every few moments for as long as it takes you to open the bottle of burgundy and taste a little. Be confident in your choice and taste the wine more than once. After quenching your thirst for the better things, add the wine to the pot along with the green peppercorns and bay leaf. Let the sauce reduce moderately by 2/3rds. Stir the veal demi-glace into the pot and season with salt to taste. I have omitted the Tablespoon of Balsamic syrup from the above ingredient list. But I do indeed add it for many reasons. Just curious to see who is paying attention?

To rectify your friend's adoration of your skills as a cook, pre-heat the oven to 400 degrees and turn the fryer on to 350 degrees at the same time. Season the marrow with some salt and pepper. Place the bones into a baking dish and roast for 10-12 minutes. The marrow should be brown and starting to slightly bubble. While the marrow is roasting, roll some of the beignet dough out to a ¼ inch thickness and cut into whatever shape fits your mood. If you have had enough Burgundy, that mood should yield whimsical and slightly abstract shapes. Fry the dough until golden and puffy delicious and set aside to stay warm. Place a pan over high heat and add a nice pat of butter. Swirl the bubbling butter around and add the snails. Sauté for a minute and add the bordelaise sauce. Bring your pan to a simmer while you take the Bones out of the oven. Place the bones onto 4 plates and smother with the sauce. Creatively toss around some beignets with their wonderful aroma of rosemary. Present to your loved ones and toast the survival of yet another Tuesday. I pray that we all have enough couth to one day own marrow spoons.

"The only possible way bone marrow could be any tastier is if you made it illegal"
Me

Frog Legs Braised in Milk with Lemon and Laurel

Serves 4

Braising in milk is an often-neglected technique in American cooking. But I'm not really an American, I am Creole. While we hold forth the majority of the values the United States has been founded, we believe in a bit more personal excess. The Right to a great meal, The Right to a proper drink and The Right to look down on those who do not believe in the same. Separate yourself as the milk does in this recipe and you will see why exactly where the weight of values should lay in society.

1/2c bacon lardons
12 Frog legs
Flour
2c milk
1/2c Pig Foot Jelly (see recipe, substitute pork or chicken stock)
1 lemon zested
2 bay leaves
ground cinnamon
Kosher salt
Ground black pepper
A Loaf of French Bread

Take out a large skillet and put the lardons into the skillet. Turn the flame to low-medium heat and lure the fat out of the bacon while browning the cubes at the same time. Remove the bacon with a slotted spoon or tilt the skillet and drag the bacon out with the intention of leaving the fat behind. Place the bacon on a plate next to the stove. Season the frog legs with salt and pepper. Dust your legs with some flour, tapping off any excess. Turn up the heat on the skillet and add the frog legs. Brown each one on high heat for a minute or so per side. Once the legs have been browned, take them out of the skillet and place on the plate next to the bacon. Pour the milk and Pig Foot jelly into the skillet right along with the lemon zest, bay leaf and 2 pats on the bottom of a cinnamon container. Return the bacon back to the skillet and bring the liquid to a simmer. Lower the heat to medium. Reduce the milk for 15 minutes until it starts to separate and "clumps" of gold start to form. Season the liquid as needed with salt. Place the frog legs back into the skillet and cook for 5 more minutes basting them with a spoon to be sure they are moist and cooked through.

Serve the legs by placing the skillet in the center of a table encouraging people to tear the bread together and sop it into the sauce. There is no better mop than a chunk of bread.

**** A lardon is a cube of bacon. Buy bacon by the slab, not pre-sliced and then simply cut into ½-1 inch cubes.

Chapter 6: Tail
The Commandments of Cooking

No relevance can ever come from using curly parsley. Italian Flat Leaf is great for many things. Substituting Curly for Flat Leaf is not acceptable.

It is impossible to produce great cuisine amongst a mess. Your kitchen must be as clean as the "ding" that's heard when you crack a smile. That's includes your wardrobe. Don't dress like a hot mess. Respect for yourself first is a must if your going to show respect for the table.

All chef knives need to be at least 10 inches long unless you are a woman or a man that drives a Porsche Boxter.

All stirring in a pot needs to be done with a wooden spoon or a rubber spatula. Metal spoons scraping against a metal pot is akin to scraping fingers on a chalkboard. Don't be that kid, everyone hates that kid.

It is my sole personal decision to never wear rubber gloves. I am a very touchy feely kind of guy and I cannot make a personal connection with the food when I cannot feel it and it feel my touch.

Every dish should be tasted 20 times by the time it is completed. 10 times physically and 10 times mentally.

The only pepper ever used in gumbo is green. Red or Yellow peppers in gumbo are an infection caused by Yankees.

Using tweezers to garnish a dish has more physiological things wrong with it than I could possibly list on one page. Don't do it.

The only time segregation should be encouraged is with salt and pepper. Do not pre-mix.

As the tide comes in and out and the sun rises and sets, the laws of food and Mother Nature are always in flux. No measurement should ever precise unless you are baking. Baking is an unyielding freak of nature.

Sweetbread and Crawfish Terrine
Serves 12

Charcuterie encourages a direct access to everything we always dreamed our life would become. It is a technique that is only suddenly being rediscovered in today's world of "here, fast, now". It is the ancient skill of craftsmen to take the ordinary orphaned ingredients and make them the kings of the table. To not appreciate the art of charcuterie is to not appreciate the intimacy of the hands. Like cuisine, a hand is neither inherently good nor inherently bad. It is what we do with it that makes it that way. You can be assured that if a fine craftsman of cookery took time to present your table with charcuterie, it is only to strengthen the bonds of brotherhood with the best tool available—his hands. Be forewarned, one must develop their own deftness with the cutting board and what surrounds it. Or you may find yourself on the wrong end of an inherently immoral hand and the bewitching of your mate.

2 lobes of veal sweetbreads
2 qts water
½ yellow onion cut in quarters
1 stalk of celery cut into quarters
1 carrot peeled and cut into quarters
4 cloves of garlic
1c chardonnay
2t ground white pepper
1/4bu flat leaf parsley
4 sprigs of tarragon
1 bay leaf
1T Kosher salt
1lb of crawfish tail meat * (save the shells)
11 ounces lean veal ground
8 ounces of skinless salt pork fatback ground
1/4t ground white pepper
1/2t cayenne
8 dashes of Tabasco
2T fresh tarragon chopped
1/4c flat leaf parsley chopped
1lb skinless salted pork fatback sliced paper thin
Bread, Creole mustard, okra pickles, boiled peanuts(see Watermelon salad recipe)

Gather the sweetbreads, water, onion, celery, carrot, garlic, wine, white pepper, parsley, tarragon, bay leaf and salt into your favorite pot and place on the stove over medium high heat. When the liquid starts to laugh at your jokes when no one else will, you know the pot is smitten with you and is doing exactly as you wish. Lower the heat with a knock-knock joke and cover your admirer. Let the sweetbreads poach in the pot for 25 minutes. Turn off the heat and uncover the pot soothing your kitchen with the aromatherapy of succulent veal and tarragon. Remove the sweetbreads from the poaching liquid and place in an ice water bath. Strain the poaching liquid into another pot. Take the shells from your crawfish and place them into the poaching liquid. Bring the liquid to a solid simmer and reduce the liquid to ½ cups. Strain and cool the reduced poaching liquid in the cooler. When the veal is well chilled remove from the ice bath and separate the pieces of the lobe. Discard any membrane and veins from the poached veal's throat. Place the sweetbreads, crawfish tail meat, ground veal, ground pork, white pepper, cayenne, Tabasco and herbs into a mixing bowl and use it just for that. Set the mixture aside, perhaps into your cooler since you are probably moving a little slower than I. Pre-heat the oven to 350 degrees. Line your terrine mold with the paper thin slices of fatback. Let the fatback climb up the sides of the mold and overhang by a few good inches. Encase the fatback with the sweetbread-crawfish filling and drape the over hanging fatback over the top of the raw charcuterie. Cover the commodity of your inherently good hands with foil and place in a hot water bath. Place the terrine in the bath into the oven for 1 hour and 15 minutes OR until the internal temperature of the terrine is 165 degrees. Remove the terrine from the bath and uncover it. Let the terrine sit out and cool 10 90 degrees on your counter. Free the terrine from any excess liquid and place the foil back on top of the terrine. Put another tray on top of the terrine and weigh it down with some cans of vegetables that your mother-in-law left in the pantry since their not good for much else. Place the terrine with its burden of weight into the cooler to chill for at least 4 hours. Remove it from the cooler and free it from the mold. Serve it on a platter with all the proper accouterments. Let the attraction of the charcuterie lure back your good sense as you shun away any immoral advances.

*I must apologize. The use of Chinese crawfish in this recipe is forbidden. I understand that Chinese crawfish may be the only option in Portland, Thomas. But I really don't care. Send me a check and I'll send you some Louisiana crawfish. Those who are caught using such an inferior ingredient shall have their tongues vexed by voodoo, never to taste the spice of love again.

Bacon Fat Poached Lobster Tail with Pepper Vinegar Sabayon
Serves 3

Life is useless without excess. We have all experienced times of bare necessity. This recipe calls for a tub of bacon fat. Out of all of the free odd bits that you can get from a chef this is most likely one that wont be given up. I suggest making friends with a "shoemaker". A Shoemaker is any chef that is so horrible he should be making shoes instead of cooking. Any chef of that caliber surely lacks the intelligence it takes to save all the bacon fat. So either eat bacon every day until you have enough or get it from your local Shoemaker. Then invite him over to dinner. After all, a palate is a terrible thing to waste.

3 8oz Lobster Tails Shelled
1qt Bacon Fat
3 wooden skewers
For the sabayon
2 egg yolks
1/4c pepper vinegar
salt to taste

Writing this ingredient list was almost as useless as one for a tomato, mayonnaise sandwich y'all. I refuse to talk down anyone interested in my table by insulting their abilities. The technique is slightly more thought provoking, although still simple for anyone.

For the Sabayon: Put the egg yolks in a medium bowl along with the pepper vinegar. Herein lies a personality test. Your choice is to either place the bowl over a pot of simmering water and begin to whisk diligently. As any rule abiding citizen would do. Or for the cooks whose life has a few less laws, place the bowl directly over the flame. If you lead a kitchen delinquent's life be prepared to whisk harder and faster than the consequences that come from such a choice. Whisk the sauce for 3-5 minutes or until a ribbon forms when you drape the whisk over the sauce. The sauce falling from the whisk will hold a streak that resembles a ribbon.
Season with some salt and place the bowl in a lukewarm place until needed.

For the Lobster Tails: Place the fat into a medium sized pot and place the pot over a medium heat. Lay the lobster tails out flat and impale a skewer down the middle of the length of the tail. Use a temperature gauge to get the fat to the desired 180 degrees. Submerge the tails into the fat. Watch your temperature gauge and adjust the heat accordingly. Cook the tail for 8 minutes. Make sure the tail is firm to the touch. You can even check for doneness by removing the skewer and feeling if it is warm on your bottom lip.

To Serve: Slice the tail into medallions and place over any of the sides in this book. Spoon some additional poaching fat over the tail and lay a summertime blanket of sabayon over the tail. Partial covering is all that is required during the summer. Give it to the Shoemaker and pray he doesn't commit Harakiri.

Ode To The Pig: The Tail

My tail is not impressive

But it's elegant and neat.

In length it's not excessive —

I can't curl it round my feet —

But it's awfully expressive,

And its weight is not excessive,

And I don't think it's conceit,

Or foolishly possessive

If I state with some agressiveness

that it's the final master touch

That makes a pig complete.

Walter R. Brooks

Gumbo Z'Herbs with Smoked Pig Tail
Serves 10

"Everything I've ever done, Everything I'll ever do, Every place I've ever been, Every where I'm going to, Is A Sin"----**Pet Shop Boys.**

I have many a friend where these words could not ring more true. I feel it is my obligation to sway their moral compass at least one day a year. The Friday that precedes Easter Sunday, Good Friday, is a day of fasting as it pertains to the hoof and the fin. On the Thursday before Easter, Holy Thursday, the Creole homes are filled with the smells of the garden's greens as they succumb to the heat and the temptation that can only be whispered by smoked pork. Gumbo Z'herbs is the traditional dish responsible for the aroma of holiness that blankets the city of New Orleans on Holy Thursday. It is comprised of as many different greens that can possibly be foraged and simmered together with a bit of moral leniency in the form of pork.

The Creoles consider the dish "vegetarian" and within the Church's eye of good faith because the pork is used only as seasoning and then is taken out. But I consider dispensing a perfectly good piece of pork a much greater blasphemy. I, personally, am as pure as the sting of Gin with a slice of cucumber on a Sunday afternoon. So this recipe is my attempt to straighten the lives of all you other sinners out there, at least for just one day of the year.

4 Tablespoons unsalted Butter
1 yellow onion diced medium
2 stalks of celery diced medium
1 green bell pepper diced medium
5 cloves of garlic sliced thinly
2 bay leaves
10 sprigs of fresh thyme tied in a bundle
1 teaspoon of dried oregano
1 teaspoon of ground black pepper
1 teaspoon of red pepper flakes
1/4c flour
2 quarts of water
2lbs of smoked pork tails
1 bunch of collard greens washed, stemmed and chopped
1 bunch of turnip greens washed, stemmed and chopped
1 bunch of mustard greens washed, stemmed and chopped
1 bunch green kale washed, stemmed and chopped
1 bunch of spinach washed and chopped
1 bunch of Italian parsley stemmed and chopped
1 bunch of radish tops washed and chopped
1 head of green cabbage chopped
1 bunch of scallions chopped
2 ounces of red wine vinegar
1 bottle of pepper vinegar
For the Peanut "Gremulata":
1c salted toasted peanuts
2 teaspoons red pepper flakes
1 teaspoon file powder
2 Tablespoons dried onion flakes
2 Tablespoons dried garlic flakes
1 cup diced radishes left over from using the tops from above

Take a very large pot and procure a place for it on your stovetop. Place the pot over a medium flame and melt the butter in it. Add the onion, celery and green bell pepper to the pot. Season the vegetables with a sprinkling of kosher salt as any confident cook would. Stir and cook the vegetables until the onion has become slightly transparent. This should happen much quicker than your last relationship. Add the garlic and cook for another minute. Place the bay leaves, thyme, oregano, black pepper, red pepper and flour into your large vessel. Stir to be sure the flour has soaked up all fat. Turn up the heat to your stove's strongest will and pour in the water. Mix the liquid with your grandmother's wooden spoon. This is a dish of high reverence and our passage to heaven can use all the help it can get. Lay the smoked tails into the water along with all the rest of the ingredients **except** the vinegar. Bring the mixture to a low simmer before reducing the stovetop to a medium low flame and covering your pot. Coax the good desire out of your greens and pork for 90 minutes. Turn off the heat and add the red wine vinegar. Taste the Gumbo and season with more salt if your good sense tells you to. If you have no good sense, than don't ask your mate because they probably don't have any either. Too many cooks spoil the pot.

To make the Gremulata: Mix all 6 ingredients together and set aside. Yes, sometimes life presented to you is actually that easy.

To serve the Gumbo: Ladle an appropriate amount into a bowl and sprinkle a bit of the gremulata over the top and even a solid dousing of pepper vinegar. Feel free to blatantly place a pigtail in your bowl. If you can't hide anything from God, than whom in the hell cares if your friends see?

****You don't have to use all the greens I listed above. But you should use at least 5 of any green you can find. Remember, "more is more".

Oxtail Grilled Cheese Sandwich with Cognac Raisin Jam
Serves 6

I am taking inspiration from my friend Bryan Jandres at Bouchon in Yountville, "Sometimes it fun to explain, analyze and talk about wine. Sometimes its fun to just put a good bottle on the table and let it all work out". There is no pre-amble to accessorize this Oxtail Grilled Cheese with Cognac Raisin Jam. I'm just putting it out on the table and letting the silence wax the poetry.

3# oxtails
flour for dusting
olive oil for searing
1 yellow onion rough chopped
3 carrots peeled and rough chopped
2 stalks of celery rough chopped
1/4c garlic cloves
2 sprigs of rosemary
1, 6oz can of tomato paste
1c water
2c red wine
2t ground black pepper

For the Jam
1/2c water
1/2c Cognac
1/3c sugar
1 orange juiced
1c golden raisins
1, 1/4oz pack of unflavored gelatin
2t fresh rosemary minced
1 loaf of crusty multi-grain nut bread
8oz of creamy French cows milk cheese
arugula and Creole mustard vinaigrette(from the Boudin de Tete recipe)

Start off by pre-heating the oven to 325 degrees. Season the oxtails with a nice amount of salt and pepper. Powder the oxtails with the flour and a few slaps of the wrist to remove the excess. Put that enamel-braising pan you saved for months to get on the stove over high heat. Drizzle in a little olive oil and brown the oxtails on all sides. Take your time and do it in as many batches as needed to not treat the pot like the general admission section of a U2 concert. Remove the oxtails and hold aside. Let the pot continue on its angry tear as you add the onion and carrots. Cook the vegetables until brown, stirring as infrequently as possible. Add the celery, garlic and tomato paste and continue to let the pot punish the vegetables for another couple of minutes. Pour in the water and wine along with the rosemary and black pepper and take a minute to free any of the crunchy bits being held prisoner on the floor of the pot with the scraping of a wooden spoon. Place the oxtails into the pot and bring the pot to a simmer. Cover the pot if you haven't yet lost the lid and place in the oven. Let the oxtails braise for 2 hours covered then remove the lid and continue to cook for another hour. Take the pot out of the oven and let cool in the broth.

For the Jam: Bring the water, Cognac, orange juice, sugar and raisins to a simmer. Cook for 1 minute. Dissolve the gelatin in 2T of water, then add to the pot and stir until it is dissolved. Stir in the rosemary and process the mixture in a food processer. Set aside to cool.

To Assemble: Pick the meat from the bones of the oxtail and strain the braising liquid. Don't be ashamed if your laissez faire attitude permits a few cloves of garlic to miss the trap of the strainer and find it's way into the bowl with the oxtail. Lightly moisten the shredded oxtail with a little of the stained liquid and season with salt and pepper to your taste. Freeze the remainder of the liquid and be confident in knowing that you are better than most people because you have that in your back pocket for another day. There are many ways to finish this dish. Spread some of the jam onto a slice of bread and top with a layer of oxtail and cheese. Unless you're an idiot, you'll know to place another piece of bread on top. Then toast it in the oven or put it in a Panini press or slowly brown in a skillet on top of the stove—the choice is yours. Toss the arugula with the vinaigrette from the Boudin de Tete recipe and serve.

"The professional kitchen is like jail, EVERYONE but yet NO ONE should ever have to experience it."   Me

Deep Fried Popes Noses with Black Pepper Honey and Biscuits
Serves 4

Some people believe "Less is More". Well it's not, "More is More". Just for that stance alone I felt the need to guild the lily with some deep fried turkey tails. The Turkey Tails are completely luxurious with the ratio of fat to cartilage to meat. Take one assertive bite and as the juice dribbles to the tip of your chin, you will be wondering why in the hell did you have to travel to the other side of the tracks to find them. Make no mistakes; the laborers of the street are no fools. They are keeping this treasure for themselves.

8 turkey tails cut into quarters—use a good knife and show no hesitation
2c buttermilk
15 dashes Tabasco
2c flour
1T granulated garlic
1t cayenne
2T Kosher salt
Peanut oil to deep fry
***For the Honey Butter*:**
1c local honey
2T un-salted butter
2t ground black pepper
3 sprigs of fresh sage
Biscuits (see recipe below)

Combine the turkey tails with the buttermilk and Tabasco in whichever bowl you may have clean. Place the marinating bird into the fridge for 8 hours or overnight.
***To make the Honey Butter*:** Combine the honey, butter, black pepper and sage into a small pot and bring the mixture to a simmer over a medium flame. Cook for 2 minutes and set aside to cool.
***For the whole dish*:** Pre-heat you fryer or a cast iron skillet filled with peanut oil to 335 degrees. Remove the turkey tails from the cooler. In another bowl combine the flour, garlic, cayenne and salt. Mix together until harmonious. Take the turkey tails and coat them in the flour and gently lay into the hot oil to fry. Fry each batch for 6-8 minutes. The turkey should be golden and easily bobbing up to the surface from the bottom of the basket. Line a platter with the biscuits and place the tails on top. Liberally drizzle the whole platter with enough honey butter to satisfy any longings. Prepare to suck on your fingers.

****This recipe is so good, I would find it hard to look down on anyone using chicken, frog legs or even pork ribs as a substitute. Just make you cook it all long enough. Perhaps 10-12 minutes.

Dave's Heritage Biscuits
Makes a dozen biscuits

In the Sweetbread and Crawfish Terrine recipe, I explained the significance our hands play in thoughtful cooking. To quote myself again, "Like cuisine, Hands are neither inherently good nor inherently bad. It is what we do with them that make them that way". My hands make biscuits. I will be remembered by the generations that both precede and precede me for the crisp flaky exterior ultra-tender buttery interior of the biscuit that has become the reflection of my soul. Glazed with black-pepper honey butter in the style of a fine sticky bun. These biscuits are the best you ever had and they will be forever indebted to my hands that they have been able to assume their rightful sovereignty among the baked goods. It is because of these biscuits that my family, both young and old, will always remember the warmth and care of my hands.

2c flour, plus a little extra for dusting
2T baking powder
2T sugar
2t Kosher salt
1/2lb un-salted butter
1 1/2c milk
1 egg

Pre-heat the oven to 400 degrees. Combine 2 cups of the flour with the baking powder, salt and sugar in a mixing bowl and mix it up with your hands. Cube the chilled butter and sprinkle it into the flour mixture. Break the cubes up with your hands until the butter resembles that of the size of a pea that you have flattened. Form a well into the center of the flour-butter mixture and pour 1 cup of the milk into the well. Mix with you fingers until the flour has absorbed the milk. Add any extra flour as needed to bring the mixture together until it resembles a dough that is submissive and will listen to the instructions that your hands give it. Sprinkle some flour out onto your counter with a few snapping flicks of your wrist and place the dough onto the floured surface. Press the dough down with your hands until a uniform thickness is achieved of about 2 inches. Cut the dough into 12 uniform biscuits. Shape them however you see fit. Place the biscuits with their sides touching one another on a parchment paper or foil lined baking tray. In a small bowl whisk together the egg with the 1/2 cup of milk and brush the egg wash over the top of the biscuits. Place the biscuits into the oven on the center rack and bake for 20 minutes. Remove from the oven and prepare for immortality.

"Chefs do not cook because they yearn to see the smiles on the faces of the guests. They do it out of vanity".
Me

Pesole Soup with Green Tomato and Brussels Sprout Salsa
Serves 10

Look beyond what I hold in front of you. If you begin to read between the lines, the true soul of The Noble Savage will be presented to you. Whether or not you can find a Turkey Tail will have no impact on your honest or even dishonest goals for the evening. It has little to actually do with recipes. It has everything to do with accessing life's pleasures that seem to be out of reach for so many people. In my lifetime, cooking has been the easiest tool used to achieve or obtain anything I ever wanted. Both the tangible and the intangible pleasures are always within the grasp of anyone that uses the one common denominator that we all cannot live without—cuisine.

1# smoked pig tails
2 pig feet
3# pork butt cut into 2 inch cubes
½ large yellow onion diced small
1/4c garlic very roughly chopped
2 passila chiles stemmed seeded and torn
1 ancho chile stemmed seeded and torn
1T Kosher salt
1T dried oregano
1T dried chile powder
2 limes
2 15oz cans of pesole/hominy rinsed and drained
½# pork skin (see Chilaquiles recipe)
For the Salsa:
1c radishes diced small
1c Brussels sprouts sliced thinly
½ jalapeno seeded and minced
2T chopped fresh oregeno
1 green tomato diced small

An exercise in simplicity of preparation is needed in order to preserve the classic style of this dish. Take all of the pig parts you intend to use, the ones listed were the ones I had around the house, place them into a large pot with the onion, garlic, chiles, salt, dried oregano, chile powder and the zest of the 2 limes. Fill the pot with water until it reaches 4 inches above the meat and place over high heat on your stove. As the broth begins to bubble, take a trusty spoon and remove any of the foam and fat that rise to the surface. Cover the pot and let it slowly simmer for 1 hours and 45 minutes. Add the pesole/hominy to the pot to cook for another 30 minutes. Season with additional salt to taste if you sense that it needs it. Remove the feet and pick out the bones. Coarsely chop the meat of the feet and add back to the pot. You can either choose to do the same with the tails or not.
While the broth is seducing the pork, bake the pork skins in the same manner as described in the "chilaquiles" recipe. Its on this website, just look for it. Set them aside for later to be used as a garnish.

To make the salsa: Toss the radish, Brussels sprouts, jalapeno, fresh oregano, green tomato, the juice of the 2 limes and a pinch of salt together. Let the "salsa" wait for the cue at room temperature.

To Assemble: Ladle the Pesole soup into bowls for your guests and garnish with a heaping spoon of salsa and some strips of crispy pork skin. Then bathe in the success of your honest or dishonest intentions for the evening.

"Having a full plate isn't as stressful as having an empty one"
                                                         Me

Chapter 7: Skin and Sides

The Significance of a Dishwasher

The most important man in any professional kitchen is the dishwasher. The dishwasher doesn't wear a big hat or a monogramed coat. But his stature is of equal to the highest chef in the brigade. He dons the cloth of the peasant. A baseball cap with a white polyester shirt bound by metal snaps enrobes what is sure to be the most respected individual in the kitchen. Day after day preforming a sweaty unwanted job for the smallest of pittance commands respect's attention.

Sergio was my dishwasher. He was walking down the sidewalk when he saw me trying to paint the outside of my restaurant in preparation of a not so grand tightly budgeted opening. He picked up a paint roller and started working. From that day on we would never be apart. He never would take a break to partake in the daily lunch, "I eat later". He was never late or did he ever miss a day of work. He never asked for a raise, so one year I bought him a van. To instill respect and equality to the cooks, I abolished the use of chef coats in the kitchen and we all wore dishwasher uniforms. Our joint tireless work ethic and preservation towards excellence afforded us a fair amount of success. There we were, a couple of downtown kids dressed up like social elitists, noses in the air ordering all the best Restaurant August in New Orleans could cast upon our table. Nothing was too extravagant or too expensive for the guys that felt equal to everyone. Although deep down, we truly felt we had no equals.

The next night we catered the GRANDEST wedding the French Quarter has ever had the pleasure of hosting. 250 miles from home, Sergio and I with OUR brigade walked into Latrobes and you would have thought we were mafia by the way we just assumed ownership of the city as our natural rite. No cost was spared, from the indoor snowball stand, the sushi station, the dessert buffet, po-boy profiteroles to the jazz marching band. We busted our ass and etched a memory that will last in 300 people's hearts for the rest of their lives. Just like every night, as we wound down the evening and mingled with the guests that insisted on professing their love for us. I asked Sergio if he wanted a cerveza. He turned to me, "Si" with an apron that seemed to have blood splattered on the front. I asked him what had happened and he said "Nothing, cutting meat". High from the constant adoration from 300 guests I didn't question him. I knew he never butchered anything that day. The next day Sergio didn't wake up. He passed from my life in the same way that he entered it. Working hard to make our lives equal to none.

Pimento Cheese with Candied Jalapeños and Chicharron "Scoops"

Serves 2

This dish consists of 2 peasant foods in a silver cup. What else is there to say?

1# or so of pork skin
1# sharp cheddar cheese in the block form
1c red bell pepper stemmed seeded and diced small
3 ounces of cream cheese
1/2c mayonnaise
2T lemon juice
10 dashes of Tabasco
1T olive oil
1/2c candied jalapeños diced*

Pre-heat the oven to 400 degrees. Lay a piece of foil over a sheet pan. Take the skin of the pork and using your best knife cut the skin into 3 by 3 inch squares. Arrange the squares onto the sheet pan with the skin side down. Lightly salt the skins the way any sensible person with a decent amount of pride would do and place in the oven for 30 minutes. Rotate the pan after 15 minutes just in case your oven suffers from a small case of schizophrenia. Make sure all of your "scoops" are golden brown and set them aside. One would have to really dislike their parents in making the conscious decision to spit on their legacy by constructing pimento cheese with pre-grated cheddar. Make your family proud and grate the cheddar then set aside. Place a small pan over low heat and drizzle in the olive oil. Scatter the pepper into the pan, season with a touch of salt and cook until soft. Set aside to cool. Take a medium sized bowl and mix together the cream cheese and mayonnaise until it is smooth. Add the respect of your family's name disguised as freshly grated cheddar along with the lemon juice, Tabasco, candied jalapeno and softened red pepper. Add some salt if you believe it to be necessary and fold the mixture with a wooden spoon as a nod to tradition. If you are kind enough with your stirring the pimento cheese will have the confidence to stand shoulder to shoulder with the best Europe has to offer. Place the Mexican "Scoops" onto the table accompanied by the Pimento Cheese in a silver cup. For this dip has no equal.

*If you are unfortunate to live where candied jalapenos are not readily available or you're just that much of a go-getter, make them yourself. Slice some fresh jalapenos and place in a pot to which you have 1 cup of water and 1 cup of sugar with1 Tablespoon of rice vinegar. Simmer a few minutes and set aside for a day or two or ten.

Pork Skin "Chilaquiles"
Serves 5

As I continue to preach the ways anyone can find luxury and couth in the most common of places. A runny egg served to a loved one is a certain indication of sincere intentions. To then present such a Godsend with crispy Pork Skins and you just may find yourself smitten with more admirers than the week and your ability to remember names with faces allow.

1lb smoked pork skins cut into ½ inch strips
1T olive oil
½ a medium yellow onion peeled and diced
3 cloves of garlic smashed
3 dried ancho chiles stemmed, seeded and roasted over a stove flame then chopped
1 dried passilla chile treated the same way as the ancho
1t ground coriander
1t dried oregano
1t dried cumin
1/4t cinnamon
1t Kosher salt
a scant whisper of ground clove
28 ounce can of peeled whole plum tomatoes
1 cup of chicken stock
more olive oil to fry the Huevos
5 eggs
Fresh cilantro, limes, queso fresco and sliced red onion to garnish
Pre-heat your oven to 400 degrees. Lay some foil down onto a couple baking trays and arrange the pork skins on the tray. Bake the skins until brown and crispy for 30 minutes. Remove the skins from the oven and hold them aside for their pending baptism.

While the pork skins are being taught some manners by your oven, place a wide mouthed pot on the stove and ignite the flame to its fullest capability. Pour the tablespoon of olive oil into the pot and start browning the onion. After the onion is sufficiently browned, add the garlic and cook for a minute. Add the chiles, spices and oregano to the pot and cook for another 30 seconds. Pour in the tomatoes and the chicken stock. Use the back of a wooden spoon and smash the tomatoes for a little therapy. If you feel you already display a calm and inviting personality, then just leave them be. Bring the pot to a simmer and cook until half of the liquid has escaped and dissipated into the air. Blend the mixture and season with more salt as needed. If you desire to test your guests threshold of pain and pleasure add some cayenne as needed and hold the sauce aside and keep warm.

To assemble: Drizzle a tablespoon or so of olive oil into a skillet that has been placed on a medium flame. When the oil smokes add a couple of eggs and season them with a little salt. Stir the pork skins into the chile sauce until they are well dressed. Continue to fry the eggs until the whites are cooked completely. Place some of the well dressed pork skin "chilaqiles" onto a plate and top with how ever many eggs that make you feel comfortable. Using your hands, garnish with some cilantro, red onion, queso fresco and squeeze the lime like it fell from the sky. Serve and savor all the adoration.

"If your hands are too shaky to garnish a dish, you don't need tweezers, you need the Red Light district"

Me

Nam Prik Ong: Red Chile Pork, Shrimp and Okra Dip
Serves 8

You can read all the issues of *Saveur* that you like. But a third hand experience is like eating with a knife and fork or making love through an interpreter. All five senses must be engaged to capture the essence of any escapade, or at least your original outlook of that escapade. I have no troubles or prejudices in eschewing the utensils in any restaurant. My fingers reach down and retrieve the food sensually or even barbarically. In the frenzy of the moment the two are often confused.

This dish has all the pleasure of one of the lesser sins. Its spicy, sweet, tart, it has pork times 2 and you unapologetically use your hands. Of course my version gets a shot of southern refinement with shrimp and okra.

3 shallots peeled
1/3c garlic cloves
10 Thai bird chilies
2c grape or cherry tomatoes
8oz fresh shrimp diced small
8oz ground pork
2c fresh okra cut into 2inch rounds
1/4c fish sauce
3T tamarind paste
1/3c water
1/2T sugar
1 lime
cilantro leaves
local vegetables such as cucumber, endive, cauliflower, carrots all cut to be able to scoop some dip.
crispy pork skins (see pimento cheese recipe)

Start off by placing a skillet over medium high heat. Dry roast and brown the shallots and garlic in the vessel. Remove to your motor and pestle. Do the same with the chilies, and then the tomatoes. Make a paste with the firmness of your pestle and forearm. Add the shrimp and pork into your roasting skillet that is set on medium high flame and cook for a few minutes. Then accommodate your sense of smell by adding your aromatic chili paste, okra, fish sauce, tamarind, water, sugar and the zest of your lime. Let the mixture cook until it becomes a thick sauce and when your wooden spoon parts the sea of flavor the walls stand and hold true. Add a pinch or 2 of salt if needed and stir in the juice of the lime. Present the warm dip to your friends by draping some cilantro over its crown. Slice some vegetables and pile on the pork cracklins to tip the scale back in favor of justice.

****This is The Noble Savage Diet. Tell yourself it's completely carb free and lets just forget about that inconsequential 1/2T sugar.

Crisp Mustard Greens with Cane Vinegar and Pecans
Serves 4

"There is no true creation only inspiration". I read that line from an interview with Thomas Keller. The meaning is that everything has been done before. Everything we create was inspired by something we saw or tasted or smelled. I was inspired to make this from a dish I had at Dominca in New Orleans involving kale. Creole cuisine is the ultimate adapter and here is my inspiration of an Italian classic.

1 bunch mustard greens
Kosher salt
cane vinegar
spiced pecans (See Recipe In Confit Gizzard Salad)

Set one of those handy home deep fryers to 350 degrees. Clean the Mustard greens by removing the stem and perhaps cut the green once along the length. While the length of the eventual fried green might be a bit cumbersome. It will bring a touch of fun barbarism to the party like an inebriated aunt. Fry the greens in the hot oil in small batches. Toss the greens about the oil making sure it all gets cooked. Frying only takes about 15-20 seconds. Remove each batch of fried greens by placing them on a paper towel to absorb the extra oil still on the greens. Be sure to season the greens with salt while they are still hot and open to your suggestion that they taste worth a damn.

Once all the greens are fried and seasoned, shake some dashes of the cane vinegar on the greens and top with the spiced pecans. Serve warm to your friends and feel good that you provided the inspiration for that day.

"Recipes are created not invented. Artists Create, Scientists Invent."
Me

Grits a la Wop
Serves 8

New Orleans is a melding of many cultures. The Italians have laid a path that all must travel at some point or another. In Italy, polenta is cooked slowly for about the time it takes to drink 3 glasses of wine. Then it is ceremoniously poured ON THE DINING TABLE, topped with various accouterments then cut into and eaten. While I am not one for dramatics (insert sarcasm here), I couldn't help but be inspired and create our own Creole version here. The only exception is that we pour it on a fine wooden cutting board; I don't really own a "farm table".

2c stone ground grits
2c half and half
6c water
1/4lb unsalted butter
Salt to taste
2c shredded parmesan
Ragout (See recipes below)

Place a wide pot with a heavy thick bottom onto the stove. Pour in the grits, half and half, water, butter and about a tablespoon of salt. Turn the heat onto medium high and give a few stirs making sure the grits aren't clumped in the corners of the pot. When the pot comes to a simmer, turn the heat to low and cover the pot. Remove the cover and stir the pot about every 5-8 minutes. Be sure that the tip of your wooden spoon massages the bottom of the pot ensuring you have no significant amount of grits stuck and burning. After 2 glasses of wine have been drank, about 40 minutes, remove the lid and continue to cook and stir for another 35 minutes. If the grits start to get firmer than a cream soup, just simply add more hot water and keep cooking.

Turn the heat off and taste the grits. Add a proper judgment of salt. Stir in the parmesan as well. Let the pot sit for about 7-10 minutes to ever so slightly cool and firm up just a touch. Place a clean wooden cutting board in the center of your table and pour the grits right into the center. Top the grits with the ragout and serve with some bread that has been warmed and wrapped in a towel.

****You could definitely use Quick Cook grits here or even cornmeal for a more authentic polenta. The texture of both would be a bit silkier and save you about 45 minutes. Use what you have in your pantry. I consider Quick Grits to be a poor alternative lifestyle choice.

Ragout
Serves 8 over the Grits a la Wop

This recipe is a lesson in economics. A real chef never lets anything go to waste. As the pages of the calendar turn, I set aside any and all scraps, ends, pieces and parts of all meats into the freezer. The knobby ends of salami, that extra pork chop, ham hock, lamb and beef trim all get set into one bag in the freezer until it is full. Then it is thawed and braised down very slowly with a bottle of wine until succulent.

1 gallon size zip lock bag full of meat scraps
2T olive oil
1 yellow onion minced
2 stalks of celery minced
6 cloves of garlic sliced
1 large can of peeled roma toamtoes
1 bottle brash red wine
1qt of stock (Artist's choice, but if you choose seafood you're a bit questionable)
2 bay leaves
T ground black pepper
Whole Nutmeg
Kosher Salt
Crushed red pepper

It is best to use a wide bottomed pot in this execution of frugality. These instructions are relaxed enough to wear linen while cooking. Put the vessel on medium heat and cook the onion with the olive oil for a few minutes. Add the celery and cook a few minutes more then the garlic should be put in the pot for just a short amount of time. Carefully break the canned tomatoes up with your hands making sure none get on your nice pants. Then add that along with the meat, wine, stock, bay leaves and black pepper. Give about 10 good swipes of the nutmeg across your grater and bring the mixture to a simmer over low heat. Cook the ragout for 3 hours. During that time, stir and check to be sure nothing is burning on the bottom of the pot. If the mixture starts to get too thick, just add a little water.

Once the 3 hours have so quickly passed, remove the bay leaves and taste your ragout. Season with any extra salt as you see fit and even spice it up a little with some crushed red pepper. Serve over the Grits or Pasta or Risotto or sliced bread.

****Sometimes I will even buy some of the heavily discounted meat at the grocery when I see it for my freezer meat cache. More often than not, it is a wonderfully flavored piece of meat that needs long cooking and care. Perfect for Ragout.

Hogs Head Cheese Risotto
Serves 6

Patience and timing are the 2 most important ingredients to this dish. The risotto will not be creamy and luxurious without patience and the little pops of gelatinized spicy pork won't arrive at the tongue if you are lacking timing.

2T olive oil
½ yellow onion minced
T garlic minced
1 1/2c aborio rice
1/2c appropriate wine such as one from Alsace
4 1/2c pork stock (chicken stock is a fine substitute)
2T butter
Kosher salt to taste
A chunk of parmesan to shred
4oz slice of spicy hog head cheese cut into 1 inch cubes
Scallion Gremulata
1 bunch scallion sliced
1c saltines crumbled
2t fresh thyme leaves

Make the Scallion Gremulata:
Get a friend with little experience in the kitchen into the fun by making the gremulata. Making sure he doesn't chop off a finger have him cut the green onion, pick some thyme leaves and crush some crackers. Mix all of it together and send him away with some wine until you need him to garnish the dish.

Make the Risotto:
Get the pork stock hot by putting it in a pot and turning the flame to high. You want the stock to be just below a simmer on the back of your stove.

Place your nicest medium sized pot on the stove. Risotto is celebration of grandmothers and you would never toast maw-maw with a Styrofoam cup. Turn the knob to medium-low heat. Add the olive oil and let it heat for 30 seconds. Put the onions into the pot and season slightly with salt. Stir with a wooden spoon and cook the onions very slowly for 4-5 minutes. Try not to put too much color on the onions. I cant say why, it just seems like the right thing to do. Add the garlic to the pot and cook for 45 seconds. Turn the heat to high and now you can add the rice. Stir it around cooking it along the onions and garlic making sure all the grains get coated with the olive oil. Deglaze the pot with the wine and lower the heat to slightly above medium. Keep stirring until the wine has been absorbed. Take 1 1/2c of hot stock and ladle it into the rice. Stir it around diligently. Only your vigilance in stirring can coax out the rice's creamy nature. Once the liquid has been absorbed repeat your earlier action and add another 1 1/2c of hot stock. Keep stirring and cooking the risotto until that batch of stock has been taken in by the generous rice. Pour the last of the stock into the risotto and hold fast to your coarse.

When the risotto has soaked up half of that final pouring of stock, start to taste it for texture and seasoning. Add some salt with a reminder that the parmesan will add a touch more salt when it is all said and done. Continue to cook until the rice is done but not mushy. You also want the risotto to be creamy and a touch loose. Not dry and clumped like mashed potatoes. Turn off the heat and add the butter. Stir it into the risotto until it has all melted. Shave and stir in about a 1/3c of parmesan. Then with about 4 good turns with your wooden spoon, add the head cheese. Place the risotto in a serving bowl and have your novice helper who is surely drunk by now bring the gremulata back to the party and garnish the risotto. Reward everyone with your impeccable patience and timing.

****I do and don't feel bad for saying this, but you can substitute sushi rice for aborio. Sushi rice is way cheaper than aborio and almost easier to find. It is not the exact same but it is pretty close. Louisiana rice isn't the same as Valencia rice used for paella but we still use it for our jambalaya. The only reason I don't feel bad is because an Italian was the one that told me to do it.

On Curing Images and Pork

The tender image is cut thinly
and with the grain,

hung up in curing rooms or
draped over water glasses to keep out flies.

If you desire the taste for yourself,
You must pull a blade literally across the marbled heart of the negative.

Turn the skin inwards, leaving the outside to scratch
Seem bitter to strangers,
 and cover with salt of silver nitrate until fat glistens in the light.

Spoiled film smells like vinegar,
but good hygiene will seal it for a decade,
enough to last to through times of famine:
when dust closes in, obscuring the fields,
when images are coarse,
when the soldiers knock at your door
summoning you to service

Tung-Hui Hu

Crostini with Peaches, Lamb Pancetta, home-made ricotta and balsamic syrup

Serves 2 or so

After satiating my lust for the rich joys of Chinese black chicken, I decided to actually be sensible for once in my life. Being sensible falls solely on one's point of view. There in lies the beauty of being sensible. It is only regulated by your own system of justification. It is completely sensible for my friend Scott to live in the Abacos and be forced to wrangle food from the ocean because he is broke and it is illegal for him to work there. Why does he insist on living a "sensible" lifestyle where he must tie a twine around his hand and pray a fish engulfs the lure he has set forth in order to eat? Love, that's why. To drop all for love could possibly be the most sensible thing that I have ever been witness to.

Well, I love not being broke. So my next recipe took into account what was fresh and inexpensive. It serves as a great Hors D'oeuvres for some friends or a bedtime snack to share with who you are in love with. Unfortunately, you will need the slightest bit of income for this dish. Since it can't be wrangled from the sea. How unromantic!

For the Ricotta:
½ gal whole milk
2 lemons juiced
1T white vinegar
kosher salt
1T fresh chopped rosemary
1T extra virgin olive oil
For the balsamic syrup:
12oz bottle of balsamic vinegar
2T dark brown sugar
To Assemble:
1 loaf crusty sliced bread
Olive oil
A few local peaches
Browned cubes of lamb pancetta (see recipe) or
High quality salumi such as Armandino Batali in Seattle
Baby arugula

To make the ricotta: place the milk in a pot and adjust your flame to medium heat. Raise the temperature of the milk to 170 degrees. Pour in the lemon juice and vinegar with a pinch of salt and stir for a brief second to just let it know that you haven't abandoned its needs. Let the milk sit for a few minutes as the curds and the whey separate. Gently ladle all the curds into a cheesecloth-lined colander and place that over a bowl to drip. Put it in your refrigerator for 6 hours or overnight to continue to drain a bit more. Remove the ricotta from the cheesecloth hammock and stir in the rosemary and olive oil. Taste the cheese and add some more salt as needed.

For the Balsamic Syrup: place the 2 ingredients into a small pot and bring to a simmer over medium-high heat. Reduce the vinegar by half. The bubbles will turn large and thick. Set into a jar until needed.

To assemble the Crostini: pour a generous amount of olive oil into a skillet and heat it on medium high until it starts to smoke. Place a few of the slices of bread into the skillet and brown on both sides. Keep repeating until all the bread is gone. Maybe drink a little wine to keep your constitution happy while you preform the mundane act of repetition. Pile all the crostini onto a plate and set aside. Peel, core and slice the peaches. Set them aside and lick your fingers confirming your sexuality. Slice your salumi as paper thin as possible and dress your arugula with some olive oil and salt. There is nothing sadder than a dry green that longs for a kiss of olive oil. Lather the ricotta onto the crostini, lay a peach slice or two, a salumi slice or two and/or some of the lamb pancetta, some loved on arugula and a drizzle of the balsamic syrup. Repeat as much as you like or at least until you get bored because you drank all the wine.

"One day you're drinking the wine, the next day you're picking the grapes"
                                        Me

Okra Pepperonatta
Serves 8

I am a sweet and spicy fiend. This recipe has everything needed to Tango all the richness associated with frying a rolled and stuffed pig face. Bet you don't hear that everyday. But wish you did.

1 red onion peeled and sliced
1 red bell pepper cored and sliced
1 yellow bell pepper cored and sliced
1 poblano chile cored and sliced
2T garlic sliced
2T tarragon
1/4c rice vinegar
1c pickled okra cut into halves

Place a large skillet onto your stove and turn the heat up as high as the fire department will allow. Drizzle a tablespoon of olive oil into the pan and place the onion into the pan. Brown the onion that you so intelligently seasoned in the skillet. Take the cooked onion and place it in a mixing bowl. Then repeat this step with the red and yellow bell pepper. Once again bring some olive oil to smoke in your hot pan and add the poblano. Cook for a few minutes and then add the garlic and the tarragon and continue to shake the pan over the heat for another 30 seconds. Take the cooking vessel off of the heat and pour in the

100

rice vinegar. Swirl around the pan and empty the contents into the bowl with the onion and sweet peppers. Toss to marry all the flavors and add any salt as needed. Set the pepperonatta aside and serve room temperature.

****The point of cooking the peppers separately is so that their individual flavor remains separate. When you eventually put down your wine glass and eat the peppernotta all the different flavors will be popping around your palate.

Succotash Salad with Cornbread Crostini
Serves 8

Perspective is always an interesting angle. What is right for one is not right to another all depending upon personal perspective. I have used this theory on many occasions to bail me out of moral dilemmas. You can look at Succotash Salad up, down and side to side and there aint nothing wrong with that. When the dish is stewed all together in a pot the flavors meld and become one. The ingredients in this salad are cooked separately so that the individual flavors POP in your mouth.

1 yellow onion medium sized, small dice
3 garlic cloves chopped
2c black eye peas (raw and fresh, frozen will pass)
2c purple hull peas (raw and fresh, frozen will pass)
2c lima Beans (raw and fresh, frozen will pass)
2 bay leaves
10 sprigs of thyme ties with a string
1 1/2qts chicken or pork stock
Kosher salt
olive oil
1 red bell pepper seeded, small diced
1 poblano seeded, small diced
2 ears of shucked fresh corn
½ red onion minced
2c grape tomatoes sliced in half
2T garlic minced
2T fresh thyme leaves
1/2c flat leaf parsley chopped
1/3c cane vinegar
2T fresh cracked black pepper (not ground)
T sugar
Cornbread Crostini (see recipe)

Retrieve a medium sized stainless steel or enamel pot from the cabinet. Cast iron or aluminum will leave a greyish hue to the beans and we want to retain our look of youth as long as possible. In the true fashion of *Grand Mere,* place the yellow onion, garlic black eye peas, purple hull peas, lima beans, bay leaves, thyme and stock of choice into the pot and bring it to a simmer on top of your stove. Cook for 15-20 minutes. Taste the beans to check for tenderness. Continue to cook or not. That part is common sense.

While the beans are cooking, place a large skillet on high heat. Coat the hot skillet with some olive oil and when its smoking add the red bell pepper. Season the pepper with a pinch of salt. Taking the definition of SAUTE quite literally, make that pepper jump around the pan. Toss the pepper around then let it sit untouched for 20-30 seconds. Do this for 2 minutes. The goal is to just put a little color on the pepper and not cook it until it is completely soft. We still want the pepper to resist our bite with a snap of its own. Place the charred bell pepper in a large bowl. Using the same skillet, repeat the process with the poblano. Put it into the bowl with the bell pepper. Use that skillet one more time and repeat the process with the corn. Cook the corn an extra minute so that it is fully cooked and its natural chalky starches have given way to its natural silky sugars. Slide the corn out of the skillet and into the bowl with the peppers. Add the red onion, tomatoes, garlic, thyme, parsley, cane vinegar, pepper and sugar to the bowl. Drizzle in 1/3c extra virgin olive oil to the salad.

There is no particular precise time to marry the cooked beans with the rest of our salad. Once the beans are cooked, drain them and remove the strung thyme along with the bay leaves. Place the beans into the bowl.
Once all of our ingredients are now ready to mingle in the bowl, toss them around. Taste and add salt to taste. If the mixture tastes too acidic, add a bit more olive oil. Let the mixture sit in the refrigerator for at least 1 hour. This will allow the aggressive raw ingredients to calm down a bit as well as chill the salad.

For the Cornbread Crostini: Take a loaf of chilled cornbread and slice into 1 inch thick pieces. Chilling the cornbread makes it easy to handle, we all seem to come apart when we are a little too hot. Pour 2 tablespoons of olive oil into a hot non-stick skillet on a medium high flame along with 1 tablespoon of unsalted butter. When the butter is foamy add the cornbread slices to the pan and brown on both sides. If the skillet appears dry before turning the cornbread's other cheek, simply add more oil.

***Corn Bread Recipe:
Chef Marco Pierre White, one of my HUGE heroes, caught a bit of lip from his detractors for his kitchen never personally making the bread at his 3 Michelin starred restaurant. Chef White would buy it from a baker in the area. "Why would I do anything, if I can pay somebody to do it better"?
For making cornbread, just buy one of those .99c packs of cornbread mix and follow the instructions. I always go for one that promotes "honey" on the label. Americans are addicted to sugar and I am American---although I deeply long to be Marco Pierre White!

Dirty Mix
Serves 6

This mix stems from "Dirty Rice". It is all the fun parts of the chicken that have been ground and spiced. I use this mix in a number of things besides the classic rice.

2T olive oil
½ yellow onion minced
1 stalk of celery minced
1 small green bell pepper minced
2T garlic minced
1T dried thyme
2t dried basil
2t dried oregano
2t cayenne
1t clove ground
1t allspice ground
1lb chicken gizzards ground
1/2lb chicken livers ground
Kosher salt
8 dashes of Tabasco
1 bunch scallion chopped
1/4c Flat leaf parsley chopped

Set a pan over high heat and add the oil. Place the onion into the pan and sauté for 2 minutes. Add the celery and bell pepper to the pan and continue to cook for another 3 minutes. Toss the garlic along with the dried herbs, cayenne and spices into pan along with the gizzards and livers. Cook for 10 minutes until cooked through. Splash the mixture with the Tabasco and season with salt and pepper to taste. Stir in the green onion with the parsley. Set aside and use at your own discretion.

For Dirty Rice: Stir in 2c of uncooked rice to the mix and sauté for a minute. Pour in 4c of chicken stock and bring to a simmer. Taste the liquid and add salt as needed. Turn the heat to low and cover the pot. Cook for 18 minutes. Uncover and serve.

For Dirty Benedict: Place the warm Dirty Mix on a toasted slice of French bread and top that with a poached egg and béarnaise as I have described in the Hog Head Benedict Recipe earlier in the book.

For Dirty Boy: Take the dirty mix and stuff it in some French bread to make a Po Boy. Dip or smother in gravy to guild the lily.

"Some of the people that are obsessed with food go to eating disorder clinics, the rest of us become Chefs"
Me

Chapter 8: One Final Dessert Recipe

Lard Cookie and Salted Dulce de Leche Ice Cream Sandwiches
Serves 7

I am a huge aficionado of salty-sweet desserts. It's a fine play that isolates the best aspects of life. No life can be balanced without disappointment, for that I do appreciate bitter. But only in small amounts that I can pawn off on other people in the way any good friend would. This recipe for an ice cream sandwich has all the best life has to offer with none of the consequence that accompanies being bitter.

For the ice cream
1 14ounce can of sweetened condensed milk *or* the same amount of already prepared dulce de leche
2c half and half
1 1/2t Kosher salt
1/4c dark brown sugar
For the cookies
1c rendered pork lard
1/2c white sugar
1/2c dark brown sugar
pinch of salt
1/2t vanilla extract
1T fresh thyme leaves
1 egg
2c cake flour

If you possess a "do it yourself" type of personality, then take the can of condensed milk and boil it covered in a pot for 2 hours. Just to have a properly stocked pantry you should probably do a few extra cans at the same time. Let your imagination run wild as to the reasons of "why". Combine one can of the dulce de leche with the half and half, salt and sugar in a stainless steel saucepan. Place over some decent heat and stir until you are confident that the ingredients have become homogenous. Chill the ice cream base and churn in your machine as you feel is best. Does anyone actually read the instructions? Place the churned iced cream into a container and place in the freezer. Go ahead and lick the churned paddle. You shan't let a drop of anything this good go to waste.
To make the cookies: Pre-heat the oven to 325 degrees. Place the lard, sugar, brown sugar, salt, vanilla and thyme in a mixer. Mix for a minute then add the egg and flour to the mix. Continue to let the machine stir for you until the dough comes together. Divide the dough into 16 balls onto a couple of greased baking sheets. Slightly flatten the balls and bake in the oven for 12 minutes. Rotate the pans to ensure all the cookies get treated equally and bake another 12 minutes. Let cool.
To assemble the ice cream sandwiches: Come on, really???

"I have made a lot of poor decisions when it comes to women, but I've never regretted dessert"   Me

To reach me and talk about Life, Love and all matters of the Table:
TheRooterToTheTooter@Gmail.com

Made in the USA
Middletown, DE
16 December 2019

80916871R00060